WHAT I'D
Say to the
MARTIANS

ALSO BY JACK HANDEY

WHAT I'D
Say to the
MARTIANS
And Other Veiled Threats

Jack Handey

New York

The following pieces were originally published in *The New Yorker:* "Job Rejection," "Thank You for Stopping," "Ideas for Paintings," "What I'd Say to the Martians," "Lowering My Standards," "My Nature Documentary," "This Is No Game," "Stunned," "My First Day in Hell," "Animals All Around Us," "The Voices in My Head," "Reintroducing Me to My Habitat," "Tattoo."

The following pieces were originally published in *Outside* magazine: "How to Prepare a Wild-Caught Rabbit for a Meal," "The Respect of the Men," "The Greatest Fly Fisherman I Ever Knew (My Hero)," "In Praise of the Human Body," "Mount Everest (30 Times)," "My Favorite Thing," "The Corrector."

"Scary Skeleton" was originally broadcast on Public Radio International's *Studio 360*.

"Legend of Me" first appeared in *McSweeney's Internet Tendency*.

The following were originally broadcast on NBC's *Saturday Night Live*: "Fuzzy Memories"; "Deer Heads"; "Anne Boleyn"; "Unfrozen Cave Man Lawyer"; "Toonces, the Cat Who Could Drive a Car"; "Happy Fun Ball."

"Some Funny New York Things" was originally published in *Los Angeles Times's Calendar* magazine.

Excerpts from *Fuzzy Memories* copyright © 1996 by Jack Handey, reprinted with permission of Andrews McMeel Publishing.

Deep Thoughts are reprinted from *Deep Thoughts* by Jack Handey, copyright © 1992 by Jack Handey. Used by permission of Berkley Publishing Group, a division of Penguin Group (USA) Inc.

Library of Congress Cataloging-in-Publication Data is available upon request.

ISBN: 978-1-4013-2266-3

Hyperion books are available for special promotions, premiums, or corporate training. For details contact Michael Rentas, Proprietary Markets, Hyperion, 77 West 66th Street, 12th floor, New York, New York 10023, or call 212-456-0133.

Design by Renato Stanisic

FIRST EDITION

10 9 8 7 6 5 4 3 2 1

To Martita

Acknowledgments

Heartfelt thanks to all the friends and colleagues who have given so generously of their time and energy over the years to review, edit, and encourage my writings. Special mention should go my tireless testers, Tom Gammill, Bill Novak, and Max Pross. Thanks also to Kit Boss, John Fortenberry, Chris and Maria Hart, Pat and Anne Marble, George Meyer, and Jennifer Meyer, as well as Dave and Sue McIntyre; Linda, Lev, Ben, and Jesse Novak; Michelle Stockwell; Rhys Thomas; and David Tomlin.

Sandy Frazier, without your steadfast support and assistance I'm not sure this book would have come into being. So if people hate it, is it okay if I blame you?

It has been a pleasure to work once again with my gracious and discriminating book editor, Leslie Wells. Generous and overdue thanks also to my editor at *The*

New Yorker, Susan Morrison, and my editor at *Outside* magazine, Mary Turner.

I am indebted to Lorne Michaels for letting me use my TV stuff in this book, and also for running probably the only show where a writer like me could thrive. And also for the great parties.

Thanks to Kurt Andersen, David Krasnow, and Peter Clowney at *Studio 360* for putting me on such a classy radio program. And with cool sound effects, to boot.

Thanks to all the people at the Andrew Wylie Agency, including the eponymous (a word I never thought I'd be able to use) Andrew, Jin Auh, Jackie Ko, and Angelin Borsics.

Cheryl Weatherby, thanks for all your hard work typing the manuscript. Appreciation also to Senior Production Editor Kevin MacDonald and the Hyperion copyeditors for catching all my misteaks.

I am withholding thanks to my cats Romero, Little Girl, and Preston. Not only have they not been particularly helpful in the writing of this book, they usually lay right on top of something I am reading or step on the computer keys.

No amount of thanks is withheld for my wife and editor, Marta Chavez Handey. Her help and support on this book, and all the pieces in it, has been invaluable. Thanks, Patita!

Contents

WHAT I'D
Say to the
MARTIANS

How Things Even Out

Things tend to even out. Religion, some people say, has caused wars and fighting. Yes, but it's also boring to sit through a church service, so it evens out. One moment you're depressed because your doctor tells you that you have alcoholism. But then you cheer up when you go home and find a hidden bottle of vodka you had forgotten about.

Things are evening out all the time, if you take time to notice, like I do. Let's say you want a big cupcake, with lots of icing, so you go buy one and eat it. But then you realize, I don't have the cupcake anymore. Or maybe you take a bite of salsa that's labeled HOT, and it doesn't seem that hot, but then about a second later it seems *really* hot.

You might hear that some guy you know is having a party, so you call him up, but he says there's no party.

But then you call back, using a different voice, and suddenly there is a party.

One day you ask people to take a look at a skin rash you have. Then a few days later you're looking at *their* rashes. You send someone a death threat and then, mysteriously, the police come to your house and threaten *you*.

Maybe you find a nice flat pebble on a riverbank, and when you pick it up and throw it, it skips across the water several times. But then the next pebble you can't even pry loose because, what is this, glue mud? You notice an ant drifting away on a leaf in the water. Then you look up to see your aunt, drifting away in a rowboat.

Eventually, I believe, everything evens out. Long ago an asteroid hit our planet and killed our dinosaurs. But in the future, maybe we'll go to another planet and kill their dinosaurs.

Even in the afterlife things probably even out, although I can't imagine how.

Still don't believe that things even out? Try this simple test: Flip a coin, over and over again, calling out "Heads!" or "Tails!" after each flip. Half the time people will ask you to please stop.

Once you realize that things even out, it's like a light being turned on in your head, then turning off, then being turned to "dim."

Probably the perfect example of things evening

out happened to me just last month. I was walking to the post office to mail a death threat. It was a beautiful day. I was happily singing away in my super-loud singing voice. I didn't step on any chewing gum, like I usually do, and when I threw my gum down, it didn't stick to my fingertips. As I rounded the corner there was a bum begging for change. I was feeling pretty good, so I gave him a five-dollar bill. At first I tried to make him do a little dance for the five dollars, but he wouldn't do it, so I gave him the five dollars anyway.

Not long after that I was reading the paper, and there was a picture of the bum. He had won the Nobel Prize in Chemistry! He had a little bigger nose and straighter teeth, but I'm pretty sure it was him. So, my five dollars had made him change his ways and become a chemistry guy.

A few days later I was walking by the corner again, and there was the bum, back begging. So, things had evened out. He had gotten the Nobel Prize, but now he was a bum again. I asked him for the five dollars back, but he started saying weird stuff that I guess was chemistry formulas or something.

I told my friend Don the story, but he said it wasn't an example of things evening out so much as just a stupid story. That's interesting, Don, because you saying that evens out what I said to your mother that time.

I have a lot of stories about things evening out, but I think the one about the Nobel Prize–winning bum is the best. I'd say it would take about three of my other stories to even out that one.

Job Rejection

Dear Sir:
A few days ago, you phoned us about the job you applied for with our company, and we told you that you did not get the job. However, we are now writing to inform you that you did not get the job. We wanted to make sure you understood that.

Sincerely,
Personnel Department

Dear Sir:
Congratulations! You got the job! That is probably what you were hoping this letter would say. But it doesn't, because you didn't.

Sincerely,
Personnel Department

Dear Sir:

You recently applied for a position with us, but you did not get it, as we have informed you by phone and by mail. However, we have not heard back from you that you completely understand that you failed to get the job. Please call or write and let us know that you realize that you are not employed by us in any way, and never will be.

Sincerely,
Personnel Department

Dear Sir:

Please be advised that the person we hired instead of you has been promoted to department manager, and he has asked us to inform you that, should a position open up, he would not hire you.

Sincerely,
Personnel Department

Dear Sir:

Would you consider taking a job for less pay than we originally discussed, even though we would never offer you such a job?

Sincerely,
Personnel Department

Dear Sir:

If it is any consolation, we feel that if we had hired
you, by now we would have been forced to let you go.

Sincerely,
Personnel Department

Dear Sir:

We are writing to find out what kind of carpeting and
curtains you want in your new office. . . . Wait, we made
a mistake. You're the wrong person. Oh well, we're going to go ahead and send this letter to you anyway.

Sincerely,
Personnel Department

Dear Sir:

Could you report for work first thing Monday morning, if you had a job? Just curious.

Sincerely,
Personnel Department

Dear Sir:

While updating our file of job applications, yours was
folded into a paper airplane and was accidentally
flown out the window. Would you mind filling out
the enclosed application and mailing it back to us in
the shape of an airplane?

Sincerely,
Personnel Department

Dear Sir:

As you may have read in the newspaper, our company has been crippled by a union strike, and we have had to call in outside, freelance help, for which we are paying many times the normal salary. We just thought you should know that.

Sincerely,
Personnel Department

Dear Sir:

It has come to our attention that an employee in our department has been sending you unauthorized and inappropriate letters. We have told him not only that he is fired, but that we are hiring you in his place. He left here in an uproar, swearing that he was "going to find [you] and crush [your] head like a walnut." (Some of us think he said "like a peanut," but most think he said "walnut.") If he shows up at your apartment, please explain to him that we were just kidding; we would never hire you.

Sincerely,
Personnel Department

Thank You for Stopping

Thank you for stopping. You have obviously found me unconscious by the side of the road, or at a party, or possibly propped up against a wall someplace, and you have wisely reached into my pocket and found this medical advisory.

If you found other things in my pockets, kindly do not read or keep them. They are none of your business and/or do not belong to you. And remember that, even though I am unconscious now, when I wake up I will remember the things I had.

If I am wearing a tie, please loosen it. But, again, do not take it off and keep it. It is not yours, and is probably more expensive than you can afford. If I am not wearing a tie, look around at the other people who have gathered to look at me and see if one of them is wearing a tie that might belong to me. If so, please approach that individual and ask for my tie back. If he says it is his, say you do not think so. If he insists, give him one of the cards (in the same pocket where you found this note) of my attorney, and tell the person he will be hearing from him soon.

Keep me warm. Take off your coat and put it around me. Do not worry, you will get it back. If you do not, within thirty days contact the attorney on the card, and he will advise you.

If you must, build a fire to keep me warm. But—and this is very important—DO NOT ROAST ME OVER THE FIRE. I say this because many people who stop to help others are not that smart and are capable of doing such a thing.

There are some pills in one of my pockets. Take them and hold on to them. If any authorities ask you about them, say they are yours.

If I am outdoors under a hot sun, do not allow children near me with a magnifying glass. Even if they are on leashes, do not allow monkeys near me. Do not allow others to make fun of me, poke me with sticks, or, if an anthill is nearby, pour honey on me. Do not allow onlookers to pose with me for "funny" photos. Failure to stop any of these things may be construed as participation in them, and may subject you to severe legal remedies.

Try to keep me calm. If you are not a physically attractive person, try not to let yourself be the first thing I see when I wake up.

Call an ambulance. I guess that would be obvious to most people, but you never know.

If I am on fire, put me out. If you put me out by rolling me on the ground, do not let me roll down a hill. If I do roll down a hill and get stuck under some bushes, just leave me there; you've given me enough "help" already.

If I suddenly begin to sweat profusely and my entire body begins to shimmy violently, do not worry; that is normal.

If I am bleeding, how'd that happen? What did you do now?

Even though I am unconscious, do not dangle things over me. I do not like that.

Answer my cell phone if it rings. If it is a woman named Peggy, pretend to be me and say you are breaking up with her.

If I have wet my pants, get a glass of water and act like you tripped and spilled it on me.

If I appear near death, do not call a priest. And do not call a rabbi and a minister, and have them all go into a bar and do something funny, because I don't want my life to end up as one big joke.

Get a better job. If you have time to stop for unconscious people, you are obviously not working at full capacity.

Thank you again for stopping. Now, please, stand back and give me some air.

Ideas for Paintings

Because I love art, I am offering the following ideas for paintings to all struggling artists out there. Some of those artists may be thinking, Hey, I've got good ideas of my own. Really? Then why are you struggling?

These ideas are free of charge. All I ask is that when you have completed a painting, as a courtesy to me, you sign it "Jack Handey and [your name or initials]." And, if the painting is sold, I get approximately all the money.

Good luck! Let's get painting!

STAMPEDE OF NUDES

The trouble with most paintings of nudes is that there isn't enough nudity. It's usually just one woman lying there, and you're looking around going, "Aren't there any more nudes?" This idea solves that.

What has frightened these nudes? Is it the lightning in the background? Or did one of the nudes just spook? You don't know, and this creates tension.

MADE YOU LOOK
This idea is difficult to execute, but could be a masterpiece. It depicts a grandly dressed lady, looking straight at you. At first her look seems to say, "Quick, look behind you!" So you turn around, and when you look at her again, her expression now seems to be one of smug satisfaction.

THE BLEAK HOTEL
A man is looking out the window of a bleak hotel room. He looks depressed. From the side, flying through the air, is a football. And you realize, if he's depressed now, just wait until he gets hit in the head by that football.

THE REPENTANT CAMERON DIAZ
Cameron Diaz, her tear-streaked face lit by a candle, gazes wistfully at a picture of me.

THE WEARY PEASANTS
Some tired-looking peasants are walking down a road at sunset, carrying sheaves of wheat. A nobleman in a fancy coach is coming up from behind. This makes for drama, because you're thinking, Why don't those peasants get out of the way?

SELF-PORTRAIT WITH STARTLED EXPRESSION
The key here is to be able to constantly startle yourself as you're painting. One option is to hire a startler, but that can get expensive. (The best ones are from Ireland.) Be sure to use opening the bill from your startler as a free startle.

ABSTRACT WHITE #1
This is a solid-white painting. You might be asking, "Is it okay to put in a fleck of color here and there?" I give up, do whatever you want.

THE BOXERS
Two boxers are whaling away at each other in a boxing ring. But then you notice that the people in the audience are also fighting each other. And it makes you question who are the truly barbaric ones here, the boxers or the spectators? Then you can turn the painting over and read the answer: "the boxers."

THE FRENCH LOVERS
A French dandy is embracing his beautiful buxom lover in a lush, overgrown garden. This painting should be in the shape of binoculars.

STILL LIFE WITH RABBIT
A wooden table is chockablock with fruit, cheese, and a glass of wine. To one side is a dead rabbit, a dead

pheasant, and a dead eel. And you're thinking, Thanks for the fruit, but man, take better care of your pets.

STILL LIFE WITH BEETS, CAULIFLOWER, LIVER, AND LARGE GLASS OF BEER
Just kidding. Only the beer.

THE DEATH OF HERCULES
An old Hercules is being lifted into the air by angels. On the one hand, it makes you feel sad, but on the other, you think, He's still in pretty good shape.

THE JOLLY DANCER
The scene is a flatboat on the Ohio River. A frontiersman who looks like me is doing his funny cowboy dance. Everyone seems to be enjoying the dance except for an insane simpleton who looks like my so-called friend Don. Crawling up behind Don is a big snapping turtle.

UNTITLED
This can pretty much be anything. Just remember to make it good and to put my name on it.

Scary Skeleton

I suppose we all have the same dream: a hundred years from now, a man carrying a lantern enters a darkened tomb. He's already nervous, and he hears something behind him. He turns and holds up the lantern. It's a hideous skeleton! Speechless with fear, he stumbles backward. He trips, dropping the lantern. The oil spills and catches him on fire. A flailing fireball, he runs from the tomb, into the night.

You may be asking, Why do they still have oil lanterns a hundred years from now? Look, I think you're missing the point. The point is, after you die, you want to have a scary skeleton. You don't want to be discovered by a grave robber or an archaeologist or a jogger and have the guy shrug and go, "Well, here's another one."

Why a scary skeleton? First of all, because it's scary. It scares people. If a skeleton's not scary, what's the point of even having one? Also, scariness can actually protect your skeleton. Something like half of all skeletons are eventually dug up and sold. Some go to medical schools, or are taken apart and used as musical instruments. Even worse, many end up in teenagers' bedrooms, where they are propped up in chairs with funny hats, "smoking" a cigarette. Remember: a scary skeleton is a safe skeleton.

But scary skeletons don't just pop out of the ground. Or if they do, a lot of planning was involved. Some people make the mistake of thinking that just because they're hideous in life, their skeletons will be hideous. Unfortunately, that's a myth. There are no easy skeletons.

Probably the most obvious way to make your skeleton scarier is to gradually distort your bones into grotesque shapes while you're still alive, using a series of heavy vises and clamps. But this is not as easy as it sounds; you may just wind up with an expensive set of clamps. The truth is, the time to consider this method is probably when you're young and your bones are pliable. But most people don't even think about their skeletons then. They're too busy going, "Oh, let's play hide-and-seek" or "Oh, where's my dolly?"

An easier, more practical alternative might be to have your eyeballs injected with some sort of preservative after you're dead. That way, your skeleton will have intact eyeballs, which is very scary.

You may be wondering if some sort of insect larvae could be injected in your eyes, so worms or whatever could wiggle out. I think maybe you're overthinking it. The odds of that happening at the exact right moment are almost nil.

To me, the best ideas are simple. This guy I met in a bar said to just bury the body with a knife in its hand. A skeleton holding up a knife is pretty scary. But wouldn't the knife just fall out of the guy's hand? said this other guy in the bar. Not, said the bartender, if you secured the knife to the hand with some bolts and wing nuts. Simple, clean, scary. And it leads to other ideas: Could there be some sort of spring mechanism so that when the coffin lid is opened, the skeleton actually makes a stabbing motion? And what would the warranty be on such a mechanism? These are all questions best discussed with a qualified funeral director.

It will probably take Congress to deal with some issues, such as if a skeleton should be allowed to have a loaded gun. On the one hand, an armed skeleton is scary, no doubt. But what if a dog digs up your skeleton? Even if the dog doesn't get shot, it could drag the skeleton around as it fires randomly in all directions. And no one wants to see that.

I wish there were some magic formula for producing a scary skeleton. A lot of times it comes down to common sense. A terrifying skeleton that instantly crumbles into dust, and then the dust is blown away by a special fan that runs on solar power, might sound good on paper. But in the end, a few nails pounded into your skull at the right angles might be more effective.

The main thing is, try to avoid clichés. You can have your teeth sharpened and let your fingernails grow long, but really, is that the best you can come up with? Here's an easy test: Ask yourself what you find scary in a skeleton. Or ask your kids or your grandkids. Then "build" on that.

I can't reveal what I've decided for my skeleton, because that might hurt the scariness. All I can tell you is that if you plan on opening my coffin, you'd better bring one of those heart-reviver machines. And I guess bring a blind guy, too, to operate the heart reviver.

(AUTHOR'S NOTE: Maybe they have oil lanterns a hundred years from now because there was a nuclear war or something, and electricity became extinct.)

My Third-Best Friend

I have been saying it for so many years in private, I think it's high time I said it publicly: my wife, Brenda, is not only my wife, she's my third-best friend. That's right, of all my friends in the world—and I'm guessing if you added them up there would be more than a dozen—I rank her below only two other people.

My best friend, I would have to say, is Jerry Blake, mainly because we work together and because we eat lunch together quite a bit. Jerry and I get along very well, although sometimes he can get cranky, especially when the pollen count is high. Also, I suspect that some of the things I tell him in confidence he reports back to our boss. He's not perfect, but still, overall, I'd have to rank him number one.

My second-best friend is Pete Garcia, simply by virtue of the fact that we roomed together in college.

I haven't actually seen him in many, many years, but I get a greeting card from him and his family almost every Christmas. Sometimes I feel like calling him up and recounting some of the crazy things we did in college, but his phone number is unlisted, and I'm not sure where he works these days.

As I said earlier, my third-best friend is my wife, Brenda. One of the main reasons she is ranked so high is that she has actually saved my life on several occasions.

The last time she saved my life, we were up at Crystal Lake. I was several yards out in the water, floating on my air mattress. Brenda was onshore, preparing dinner over the campfire she had built. She was making my favorite meal, this French thing with truffles and scallops and other stuff. I can't remember what it's called, even though she's told me many times. I was relaxing comfortably, when, suddenly, I felt one of my feet slip overboard. The abrupt feeling of water around my previously dry foot caused me to panic. I began thrashing about wildly. The more I struggled to regain control of my bobbing craft, the more that very control seemed to slip away.

Finally, in a blur of white water, the air mattress flipped over. I choked and gagged, but somehow managed to maintain a grip on it. I made a bargain with God, that if He would get me out of this, I would buy a better, more stable air mattress. I cried out to Brenda.

She did not hear me the first couple of times, a fact that I still (gently) rib her about to this day.

But on the third or fourth yell, she did hear me and sprang to my rescue. She threw off her shoes, raced to the edge of the cliff, and dove in. I'll be honest, I never knew she could dive like that. She plummeted the fifty feet or so to the water in near-perfect form. I think it would have been perfect if she hadn't let her feet sort of drift apart a little bit before entry, but so what, really.

What's important is that I was sure glad to see her swimming toward me, as by now I was losing my grip on my beloved air mattress. Crystal Lake is said to be home to the rainbow trout. Several rangers swore up and down that no one had ever been attacked by any of these trout, but that's probably what they say about everything: "Oh, that bear won't hurt you"; "Oh, that beaver is harmless."

Anyway, as I held on for dear life, I thought I saw a rainbow trout right under my arm! "Whoa!" I yelled, and flung myself backward. Loss of contact with the air mattress aroused some sort of primeval flapping instinct in me. My hands and arms slapped the water repeatedly as I tried to stay afloat. The mattress seemed to drift away, as in a dream.

After what seemed like forever (although I'm sure she was actually very prompt), Brenda swam up to me. "Grab hold," she said, extending her hand.

Well, I guess I sort of lost control, because Brenda

claims I started clawing and scratching her, trying to literally climb on top of her to escape the water. I don't exactly remember it that way, but I'll take her word for it.

Finally, she "subdued" me, as she puts it, with a powerful choke hold that was, in my opinion, much rougher than necessary. I had bruises for days.

Just before we reached the shore, I guess I sort of panicked again, as I thought I heard another rainbow trout swimming right alongside of us. I managed to wrench myself free from Brenda and, I'm not sure how, make it the final few yards to land.

Still, I would have to count that as a save by Brenda, even though technically she didn't bring me all the way in.

Brenda has saved my life at least three other times, but I don't think we need to go into those times right now. The main thing is, she's very loyal and honest and sincere, all of which help her maintain that third-place ranking.

I would say my fourth-best friend is a guy named Cal down at the garage where I get my car fixed. (Cal Jenkins? Johnston?) I guess he's really more of an "associate" than a friend, because we haven't really done anything together, but he's generally friendly to me when I bring my car in, so that's pretty good.

What I'd Say to the Martians

People of Mars, you say we are brutes and savages. But let me tell you one thing: if I could get loose from this cage you have me in, I would tear you guys a new Martian asshole.

You say we are violent and barbaric, but has any one of you come up to my cage and extended his hand? Because, if he did, I would jerk it off and eat it right in front of him. "Mmm, that's good Martian," I would say.

You say your civilization is more advanced than ours. But who is really the more "civilized" one: you, standing there watching this cage, or me, with my pants down, trying to urinate on you?

You criticize our Earth religions, saying they have no relevance to the way we actually live. But think about this: if I could get my hands on that god of yours, I would grab his skinny neck and choke him until his big green head exploded.

We are a warlike species, you claim, and you show me films of Earth battles to prove it. But I have seen all the films about twenty times. Get some new films, or so help me, if I ever get out of here I will empty my laser pistol on everyone I see, even pets.

Speaking of films, I could show you some films, films that show a different, gentler side of Earth. And while you're watching the films I sort of slip away, because guess what? The projector is actually a thing that shoots out spinning blades! And you fell for it!

You point to your long tradition of living peacefully with Earth. But you know what I point to? Your stupid heads.

You say that there is much your civilization could teach ours. But perhaps there is something that I could teach you—namely, how to scream like a parrot when I put your big Martian head in a vise.

You claim there are other intelligent beings in the galaxy besides Earthlings and Martians. Good, then we can attack them together. And after we're through attacking them, we'll attack you.

I came here in peace, seeking gold and slaves. But you have treated me like an intruder. Maybe it is not me who is the intruder, but you. No, not me—you, stupid.

You keep my body imprisoned in this cage. But I am able to transport my mind to a place far away, a happier place, where I use Martian heads for batting practice.

I admit that sometimes I think we are not so different after all. When you see one of your old ones trip and fall down, do you not point and laugh, just as we do? And I think we can agree that nothing is more admired by the people of Earth and Mars alike than a fine, high-quality cigarette. For fun, we humans like to ski down mountains covered with snow; you like to "milk" bacteria off of scum hills and pack them into your gill slits. So are we so different? Of course we are, and you will be even more different if I ever finish my homemade flame thrower.

You may kill me, either on purpose or by not making sure that all the surfaces in my cage are safe to lick. But you can't kill an idea. And that idea is: me chasing you with a big wooden mallet.

You say you will release me only if I sign a statement saying I will not attack you. And I have agreed, the only condition being that I can sign with a long sharp pen. And yet you still keep me locked up.

True, you have allowed me reading material—not the "human reproduction" magazines I requested, but the works of your greatest philosopher, Zandor or Zanax or whatever his name is. I would like to discuss his ideas with him—just me, him, and one of his big, heavy books.

If you will not free me, at least deliver a message to Earth. Send my love to my wife, and also to my girlfriend. And also to my children, if I have any anyplace.

Ask my wife to please send me a bazooka, which is a flower we have on Earth. If my so-called friend Don asks you where the money I owe him is, please anally probe him. Do that anyway.

If you keep me imprisoned long enough, eventually I will die. Because one thing you Martians do not understand is, we humans cannot live without our freedom. So if you see me lying lifeless in my cage, come on in, because I'm dead. Really.

Maybe one day we will not be the enemies you make us out to be. Perhaps one day a little Earth child will sit down to play with a little Martian child, or larva, or whatever they are. But after a while, guess what happens: the little Martian tries to eat the Earth child. But guess what the Earth child has: a gun. You weren't expecting that, were you? And now the Martian child is running away, as fast as he can. Run, little Martian baby, run!

I would like to thank everyone for coming to my cage to hear my speech. Donations are gratefully accepted. (No Mars money, please.)

Lowering My Standards

As you may have heard, I have very high standards. When people see me do something, they often shake their heads in disbelief. That's how high my standards are.

But lately I've been wondering if maybe they're not *too* high. Am I pushing myself too hard? Do I always have to be the one everybody looks up to? Are my high standards hurting my happiness and things like that?

Why, for instance, do I always have to be the first one to show up at a party and the last one to leave? And while I'm at the party is it really so important that I tell the dirtiest joke? A lot of times, I'm the only one telling a dirty joke, so it's not even that big an accomplishment. And if someone else does tell a dirty joke, why do I feel compelled to tell one that is even dirtier and more graphic? Just so I can be number one?

Why do I sometimes feel like I should get "a job" or

do some kind of "work"? Does thinking about maybe getting a job make me better than other people? Am I worried that if I quit borrowing money from my friends they'll think I'm stuck-up?

Why do I have to be the honest one? Do people really want you to be that honest about how old they look or how big their breasts are?

When I catch my foot and stumble on the sidewalk, why do I have to pretend to keep stumbling, all the way down the street? To avoid embarrassment?

At every get-together, why do I have to do my funny cowboy dance? Why not do a dance that isn't so demanding, like my funny robot dance or just funny prancing?

Is it really my responsibility that half-empty glasses of beer not be wasted?

Whenever there's a scary sound at night, why do I have to do all the screaming? Maybe somebody else can scream and cry and beg for mercy, for a change.

Would the world really fall apart if I didn't point out to people which are the regular goldfish and which are the bug-eyed ones? Let them figure it out on their own.

Why does it have to be me who ends up asking how much someone paid for something? *Everyone* is curious.

Could a sock really be a parachute for a mouse? Maybe not, but does that mean I have to stand up in the middle of the movie theater and start booing?

Why do I always have to be the one who sums up what was just said, or explains to the children what Hell is, or calls the meeting to order?

These are all questions I would never even have asked myself until that incident with Don. Every day my friend Don and I would see who could trip each other the most times. But then one day I tripped him and he fell and broke his jaw. He looked up and, with slurred speech, said, "I guess you win." But what did I win? I didn't win anything, and you know why? Because I forgot to make a bet with him. But something else was wrong, and I knew it. Why did I want to trip Don in the first place? To show how clever I was, or how brave, or how successful? Yes, all of those things. So I guess that answers that.

Still, something about it bothered me. I decided to drive up to a cabin in the mountains. For a week, all I did was sit and think and watch a lot of television. How, I agonized during the commercial breaks, did I get such high standards? Was it something from my childhood, or my fraternity-hood? Was it from another lifetime, when I was in another fraternity? I wondered if my high standards were leading me to a heart attack. Then I thought, Yes, but it'll be the biggest heart attack anyone's ever had. I wondered if it was even possible for a person like me to lower his standards. Then I wondered if they still make Bosco. I became so confused and frustrated I began smashing things in the cabin. I wound up running headlong into the woods in panic when the people who owned the cabin suddenly showed up.

As I drove back to civilization (as you squares call it), I had already made a momentous decision: I would keep thinking about the possibility of lowering my standards. Maybe, just maybe, I don't always have to do things so perfectly. Maybe when I ask someone a question I don't always have to begin it with the words "Pray tell." Perhaps I don't have to wear the fanciest fanny pack that money can buy. And when I'm at a dinner party, maybe I don't need to sniff every piece of food before I eat it. In short, perhaps I should worry less about doing the right thing and more about doing the right *thang,* whatever that means.

People may worry, "Isn't there a danger that if you start lowering your standards they'll go too low?" As far as I'm concerned, they can't go low enough.

How to Prepare a Wild-Caught Rabbit for a Meal

The first thing you want to do, after catching a wild rabbit, is to calm the rabbit down. A panicked rabbit does not make for a pleasurable dining experience. It taints it. Pet the rabbit. Maybe say something soothing, like "Easy, Brownie, easy" (if the rabbit is brown) or "Easy, Gray Boy, easy" (if the rabbit is gray). You might just say, "Easy, little bunny." (But really, can't you come up with some kind of name besides "bunny"?)

Feel the belly. It should be plump and fuzzy. But skinny is fine too. Feel the ears. They should be soft and pink. Man, I love the ears.

If you like your rabbit spicy, try rubbing him with wild sage or wild mint.

Place the rabbit on a rock with good drainage. Next, take out a long, sharp butcher knife. Try not to let the rabbit see the knife. You may not want to look at the knife yourself, as some of them are kind of scary-looking.

Hold the rabbit down firmly with one hand. With the other hand, take a carrot out of your backpack. Still holding the rabbit, place the carrot on the rock and slice it with the butcher knife. Then feed the carrot pieces to the rabbit. If the rabbit doesn't eat all the pieces, feel free to eat the leftovers.

Let the rabbit go. For fun, throw the knife at a tree trunk, to see if you can make it stick, like Jim Bowie or something.

(P.S. The reason you want a rock with good drainage is in case he pees.)

My Favorite Deep Thoughts

If you ever fall off the Sears Tower, just go real limp, because maybe you'll look like a dummy and people will try to catch you because, hey, free dummy.

When I found the skull in the woods, the first thing I did was call the police. But then I got curious about it. I picked it up, and started wondering who this person was, and why he had deer horns.

It's easy to sit there and say you'd like to have more money. And I guess that's what I like about it. It's easy. Just sitting there, rocking back and forth, wanting that money.

It takes a big man to cry, but it takes a bigger man to laugh at that man.

· · · ·

To me, it's a good idea to always carry two sacks of something when you walk around. That way, if anybody says, "Hey, can you give me a hand?" you can say, "Sorry, got these sacks."

Consider the daffodil. And while you're doing that, I'll be over here, looking through your stuff.

To me, clowns aren't funny. In fact, they're kind of scary. I've wondered where this started, and I think it goes back to the time I went to the circus and a clown killed my dad.

I believe in making the world safe for our children, but not our children's children, because I don't think children should be having sex.

To me, boxing is like a ballet, except there is no music, no choreography, and the dancers hit each other.

If you ever drop your keys into a river of molten lava, let 'em go, because, man, they're gone.

One thing kids like is to be tricked. For instance, I was going to take my little nephew to Disneyland, but instead I drove him to an old burned-out warehouse.

"Oh, no," I said, "Disneyland burned down." He cried and cried, but I think that deep down, he thought it was a pretty good joke. I started to drive over to the real Disneyland, but it was getting pretty late.

Anytime I see something screech across a room and latch onto someone's neck, and the guy screams and tries to get it off, I have to laugh, because what is that thing?!

Einstein and Capone

Einstein was riding high. He had already made Newton look like a fool and was playing FDR for a sucker. Capone was a wily gangster who had figured how to turn booze and prostitution into things people wanted. Friends kept telling each of them, "You've got to meet Einstein," "You've got to meet Capone." So finally they did meet, at a costume party.

"Listen, Einstein," said Capone, who came as a hobo, "I think we should join forces. With your brains and my muscle we'll be unstoppable."

Einstein, who was dressed as Tarzan, replied, "But what about my muscles?" There was an awkward moment of silence where Capone and his henchmen stared down at the floor. One of the henchmen cleared his throat but didn't say anything.

At first Einstein and Capone didn't get along. Einstein found Capone too "brusque," and Capone was always pulling out his gun and making Einstein "dance." But eventually they formed a bond so strong that people think I am making it up.

Their favorite joke was to have someone ask them which one was Capone and which one was Einstein, and they would both point at each other. They were like a couple of slaphappy kids, going around slapping people. If you got slapped by Capone, there wasn't much you could do about it. And if Einstein slapped you, you'd go, "Wow, slapped by Einstein."

But then, things deteriorated. There was the time the two of them tried to move an upright piano up a long flight of steps, resulting in a series of setbacks and false starts. And in the end it turned out to be the wrong address. Capone grabbed Einstein by the lapels and told him never to tell anyone.

Einstein started wondering if people really believed his theories or they were just afraid of getting beat up by Capone. Capone thought Einstein lived in a dream world while he, Capone, had to put on a suit each day and go out and try to make a living.

So Einstein and Capone reluctantly agreed to part company. No one really knows what they said to each other that day as they walked through the park. But onlookers would have noticed that they took a wrong turn down a path and wound up at a dead end kind of a thing where they tried to cut through and got stuck in the branches of some shrubs. There was some cursing and a few cries for help, but then both of them finally emerged into a sort of gully area before climbing up a steep embankment to get back on the path.

Years later, when Einstein heard Capone was dying of syphilis, he cried. When Capone heard about Einstein's hair, how wild and frizzy it had gotten, he laughed. Little did either one of them know that watching them that day in the park, with a pair of binoculars, was the man who would be responsible for both their deaths: Nixon.

My Nature Documentary

Show monkey in a tree. Narrator says, "The monkey, proud and smart, in his native habitat. But one thing he does not have"—show a giraffe—"is a long neck, like the giraffe. Which is why nature has allowed them to combine forces." Show monkey on giraffe's neck. (Note: monkey may have to be tied on.)

Then the narrator says, "The monkey can now see very far, and has protection from predators. And the giraffe has a little friendly guy to ride around on him."

Show monkey shot by a poacher and falling from giraffe. Put ketchup on monkey to make him look bloody, but put something bad-tasting in the ketchup or monkey will lick it all off. Shoot BB gun at giraffe to make him run off. Narrator: "The monkey and the giraffe have been separated."

Show monkey wandering around, injured, lost, and alone. Make him trip, using fishing line attached to his leg. (Try to get shot on first take, because after that, monkey will probably try to bite off fishing line.)

Show giraffe being chased by a lion. If not too expensive, use full-sized, realistic, robotic lion, able to run at full speed. Or a man in a lion suit.

The oppressive sun beats down on monkey (heat lamp). Monkey looks up with an expression that says, "Why, oh sun, do you torment me so?" (Get good director.)

We see lion eating a giraffe. At first we think it is our giraffe, but then we are relieved to see it is a baby giraffe.

Rock slide covers monkey (fake monkey). Show monkey crawling out (real monkey with a few heavy rocks laid on top of him). Narrator: "Can the monkey and the giraffe survive? Will they ever be reunited?"

Show monkey trying to join group of monkeys (children in monkey suits). Our monkey is driven away by the leader of the monkey pack, a vicious, snarling brute (papier-mâché marionette). Subtitle translates snarls as: "You thought you were so great when you were riding on that giraffe's neck, but you aren't so high and mighty now."

Show giraffe, alone in the darkness, shivering from fear (ice packs on legs). Finally, he falls asleep. (Sleeping pills?) We see his dream. In it, the giraffe fearfully approaches a gravestone. At first he can't make out the name on it, but when he finally does, he is shocked.

The name on the gravestone reads "The Monkey." The giraffe wakes up in a cold sweat (heat lamp).

Show two female explorers swimming in a crystal-clear lagoon, so you can see they're nude. Narrator: "Meanwhile, nearby, are two explorers, Laci and Brandy." Show the explorers swimming for quite a while. Then show them getting dressed and leaving. We notice they have left a pair of binoculars behind.

The monkey is starving now. We know this because when he looks at a parrot on a branch, it turns into a roasted, steaming parrot on a branch.

Narrator: "The monkey is now at the end of his rope. So he puts his faith in the Almighty." Monkey prays. (Glue monkey's hands together.) Show monkey walking along later. (Be sure to unglue hands first.) He sees a glowing treasure chest, and opens it—it's filled with bananas. (Have choir singing in background, so you know it's from God.)

Refreshed by that good banana nutrition, the monkey heads off. For comic relief, show monkey approaching a skunk and getting sprayed. If monkey will not approach skunk, feed monkey whiskey so he will relax and go up to skunk. However, do not let him drink too much or he may kill skunk.

Show monkey finding binoculars. Monkey learns how to use binoculars. (Have plenty of film, because this may take a long time.) Monkey climbs up tree and scans horizon. We see his point of view, which finally focuses on yes, the giraffe! He screams (BB pellet) with joy.

Just then the giraffe is shot by a tranquilizer dart. We show the shooters, two trappers from a zoo. We know they are evil because we saw a part earlier where they were shooting each other with tranquilizer darts, to get high.

Cut to a truck traveling across the savanna. In a cage in the back is the giraffe, looking sad (half a sleeping pill). But then we reveal that it's not the two trappers driving the truck, but the monkey! (Note: Use cheap truck because monkey will probably wreck it.)

Show the two trappers sitting on ground, tied up. No need to show how the monkey captured them; just have one of the trappers say, "That damned monkey!"

Show monkey releasing giraffe from cage and monkey leaping onto neck of giraffe. (Note: monkey may not do this, so put monkey on giraffe neck and jerk back with harness; then show film in reverse.)

Narrator: "The monkey and the giraffe are reunited at last, as nature intended." Show giraffe trying to reach a piece of fruit high on a tree branch, but he can't. The monkey clambers up on top of his head and picks the fruit, but then eats it himself. The giraffe shakes his head and laughs. (Give giraffe something to induce choking, then dub in laughing sounds.)

Show the two female explorers returning to the

lagoon, looking for the binoculars. They can't find them, so they just decide to go swimming again.

Monkey and giraffe gallop off into sunset. Question: Would it be too much to show monkey wearing a little cowboy hat? Cute, but maybe hurts reality of the documentary.

This Is No Game

This is no game. You might think this is a game, but trust me, this is no game.

This is not something where rock beats scissors or paper covers rock or rock wraps itself up in paper and gives itself as a present to scissors. Or paper types something on itself and sues scissors. This isn't anything like that.

This isn't something where you yell out "Bingo!" and then it turns out you don't have a bingo after all and what are the rules again? This isn't that, my friend.

This isn't something where you roll the dice and move your battleship around a board and land on a hotel and act like your battleship is having sex with the hotel.

This isn't tiddlywinks, where you flip your tiddly over another player's tiddly and an old man winks at you because he thought it was a good move. This isn't that at all.

This isn't something where you sink a birdie or hit a badminton birdie or do anything at all with birdies. Look, just forget birdies, okay?

To you, this is probably all one big party. But sooner or later the party is over, and when you wake up a little kid is poking you with a stick and his mother is telling him to get away from you.

Maybe you think this is all one big joke, like the farmer with the beautiful but promiscuous daughter. But what they don't tell you is the farmer became so depressed that eventually he took his own life.

This is not some honey-flavored, sugar-coated piece of candy that you can brush the ants off of and pop in your mouth.

This is not something where you can dress your kid up like a hobo and send him out trick-or-treating, because first of all, your kid's twenty-three, and second, he really is a hobo.

This is not playtime or make-believe. This is real. It's as real as a beggar squatting by the side of the road, begging, and then you realize, uh-oh, he's not begging.

This is as real as a baby deer calling out for his mother. But his mother won't be coming home anytime soon, because she is drunk in a bar somewhere.

It's as real as a mummy who still thinks he's inside a pyramid, but he's actually in a museum in Ohio.

You go skipping and prancing through life, skipping through a field of dandelions. But what you don't see is that on each dandelion is a bee, and on each bee is an ant, and the ant is biting the bee and the bee is biting the flower, and if that shocks you then I'm sorry.

You have never had to struggle to put food on the table, let alone put food on a plate or try to balance it on a spoon until it gets to your mouth.

You will never know what it's like to work on a farm until your hands are raw, just so people can have fresh marijuana. Or what it's like to go to a factory and put in eight long hours and then go home and realize you went to the wrong factory.

Don't get me wrong. I'm not against having fun. But it has to be a controlled kind of fun, where those who are having too much fun are asked to leave, and those not having enough fun are beaten.

You're probably not even reading this anymore. You're watching one of your "television shows." You're probably laughing at a joke some man is making at his wife's expense. But trust me, one day you're going to have to get down on your knees and beg God not to split your head open with an ax, because believe me, He'll do it.

I don't hate you. I pity you. You will never recognize the magnificent beauty of a double rainbow, or the plainness of a regular rainbow. You will never understand the joy of teaching a young boy how to swing a bat, then watching him go all over the place, swinging away.

I used to be like you. I would put my napkin on my lap, instead of forming a little tent over my plate, like I do now, with a door for the fork to go in.

I would go to parties and laugh—laugh and laugh, every time somebody said something, in case it was supposed to be funny. I would walk in someplace and slap down a five-dollar bill and say, "Give me all you got!" and not even know what they had there. And whenever I found two of anything, I would hold them up to my head like antlers, and then pretend one "antler" fell off.

I went waltzing along, not even caring where I stepped or if the other person even wanted to waltz.

Food even seemed to taste better back then. Potatoes were more "potatoey," and turnips less "turnippy."

But then something happened, something that would make me understand that this is no game. One day I was walking past a building and I saw a man standing high up on a ledge. "Jump! Jump!" I started yelling. What happened next would haunt me for the rest of my days. That man walked down off that building and beat the living daylights out of me. Ever since then I've realized this is no game.

Maybe one day it will be a game again. Maybe one day we'll be able to run up and kick a pumpkin without people asking why you did that and are you going to pay for it.

Perhaps one day the Indian will put down his tomahawk and the white man will put down his gun, and the white man will pick up his gun again because ha-ha, sucker.

One day we'll just sit by the fire, chew some chewing tobacky, toast some marshmackies, and maybe strum a tune on the ol' guitacky.

And maybe one day we'll tip our hats to the mockingbird, not out of fear, but out of friendliness.

If there's one single idea I'd like you to take away from this, it's this: This is no game. The other thing I'd like you to think about is, could I borrow five hundred dollars?

(AUTHOR'S NOTE: Since finishing this article, I have been informed that this is, in fact, a game. I would like to apologize for everything I said before. But please think about the five hundred dollars.)

The Legend of Me

They say that when the October moon is full, and the swamps and meadows are covered with an eerie mist, I will put down my beer and go walking through the streets.

According to legend, my hair will stick out wildly, from lying on the couch all day. I will walk with an awkward stagger, my arms held forward. No one knows why I walk this way. Some say it is to be ready in case I trip. Others say it is to make sure I don't go face-first through a spiderweb.

When I am abroad in the land, many of the frightened townspeople report hearing a ghastly, bloodcurdling howl. This is the part of the legend that hurts my feelings the most, because I think they're talking about my singing.

Some stories claim that if you confront me during my midnight walks and chant, "Jack Handey, Jack

Handey, give me some candy," that I will give you some candy. Man, forget it. I need that candy.

I am said to prey upon young lovers, and that if I look into a bedroom window and see them having sex, I will stand there and watch with my red, flaming eyes. But I am not looking for young lovers; I am usually looking for something else, like, I don't know, my lost treasure or something. If I happen to see two people having sex, I will stay and look, for I am curious about your human ways.

They say I can turn into a bat. I can, but not very well. What I am probably best at is wandering into a party and transforming myself into someone who looks like he might have been invited. And woe to him who fingers me as an impostor, for he will be greeted by a hideous hissing sound coming from the tires of his car.

It is whispered that I can suck the blood out of you. Others say I can start to tell a joke, but then get really confused and not remember how the joke goes, and start over again and again until it drives you mad. But it's not my fault. You see, I am the offspring of an unholy union between a man and what people in these parts call a "wo-man."

Some of the townspeople believe in me, and some don't. But if I don't exist, then how do you explain the hook scratches around your car-door lock, or the coat hanger thrown in the bushes? Sadly, even those who believe in me are reluctant to loan me money.

A few say I exist, but that I'm actually dead. As evidence, they point to the old gravestone in the cemetery with my name carved on it. But I have apologized for doing that and agreed to do community service.

The truth is, I live in a weird netherworld, somewhere between the dead and those guys who are out riding their bikes, doing stuff like that.

People are always asking if there's anything they can hold up that will frighten or repel me. One is a screaming baby. The legend also mentions my fear of fire, but come on, who's not afraid of fire? Man, wise up.

To be honest, just about anything you hold up is going to frighten me. About the only thing I can think of that might not is an ice cream cone, so long as the ice cream isn't in a scary shape.

Legend says that if sunlight ever hits me, I will wither into a pile of dust. That's true.

Can I be stopped by bullets or clubbing? Of course I can! What are you thinking?! And I would appreciate it if you wouldn't shine a flashlight in my face.

How did I come to this curse? I'll tell you. I was bitten, bitten by a wolf. And not an ordinary wolf, but something called a "schnauzer." A schnauzer owned by my so-called friend Don. Ever since then I am compelled to wander the night, like a schnauzer.

They say my midnight haunts will never end until I am united with my true love. The sad thing is, I don't even know her name. It's that French girl from the movie *Swimming Pool.* But unless I can figure out the area code for France, my love is probably doomed.

Maybe magically the curse will be lifted. I'll get up bright and early and point to myself in the mirror and say, "You're going to do great things today." No, wait, that's a different curse.

And so I stalk. Usually Friday and Saturday nights are the main times I go stalking, and also, like I said, the moon should be full and mist covering things. But to be honest, it could pretty much be any night of the week.

Hitchhikers

I have a confession to make. About a year ago, I was driving along a country road when I hit a hitchhiker. That it was an accident in no way excuses the pain and suffering I caused.

About a month later, I hit another hitchhiker. A hitchhiker can leave a pretty good dent in your car, so I took it into the shop to get both dents removed. While it was there, I decided to get around by hitchhiking.

Right away, an older gentleman picked me up. He grew tired of driving, and I offered to take over. While I was driving, I hit another hitchhiker. The old man was asleep at the time, so I never told him.

Later, I heard that the hitchhiker had tracked the old man down and, when he went out to check his mailbox, drove by and hit him with his car. How the hitchhiker got a car, I don't know. Maybe it was a friend's car, or maybe his car had also been in the shop. But the point is, it's a weird world out there.

Since hitting that last hitchhiker, I have accidentally hit twenty-eight other hitchhikers. I don't know what's going on. Everyone hits at least a few hitchhikers every year, whether you realize it or not. (Have you ever been driving and hit a strange bump and wondered, What was that? That was a hitchhiker.) But, to me, twenty-eight seems like way too many.

I decided to get to the bottom of it. Maybe I was just going through a hitchhiker "phase." Or maybe it was something more serious.

My eye doctor checked my eyes and said they were fine. I asked him to also look at my car, and although he insisted that he wasn't a mechanic, he said it looked okay to him.

I wondered if I harbored some secret animosity toward hitchhikers, so I went to a psychiatrist. He gave me a test. First, he handed me a framed picture of a hitchhiker and asked me my thoughts. My first thought was to wonder why someone would frame a picture of a hitchhiker, but he wanted more. "I hope he gets a ride," I said of the picture, and put it down. Then he gave me a framed picture of a driver. "I hope he has a safe journey," I said. Then I accidentally dropped the driver picture onto the hitchhiker picture, breaking it. The psychiatrist asked me not to come back, so I guess I passed.

Has drinking been involved? Unfortunately, yes. Not prior to the accidents, but afterward. If you have ever seen the terrifying face of a hitchhiker pressed against your windshield, or heard his angry words as you sped away, then you, too, would need to go home and have a stiff drink.

Some people say, Why don't you quit driving altogether? It's funny, but after each hitchhiker you hit, you think, That's got to be the last one. Then, of course, it isn't. But even if you stop driving, you can't avoid hitchhikers. They're part of our culture. When you walk from one room to another, aren't you giving "hitchhikers" a ride? (I'm not sure, I'm just asking.)

So what can be done? I believe that, working together, hitchhikers and I can cut down on the number of them I am hitting. For hitchhikers, I would suggest:

- Don't hitchhike on a curve, because a lot of times you can't control a car when you're going around a curve, and you drift up onto the shoulder. Don't stand on a straight stretch of highway either, because sometimes the straightness can make a driver confused, and he'll start swerving all over the place.
- Don't hold up a sign, because when you read something, you naturally aim for it.
- Don't wave that thumb back and forth, because that can mesmerize a driver.

I am trying to do my part. For one thing, when I drive at night, I always make sure my lights are on. Also, I have installed a loud warning siren on my car, which I blast when I'm close to a hitchhiker. I have a lot of other ideas, which I write down on my notepad while I'm driving.

I don't blame hitchhikers. They're simply doing what nature intended. Hitchhiking is not evil, but neither is it the panacea some people think it is. I foresee a day when I will spot a hitchhiker on the side of the road, and I will wave politely as I drive by. Or I will pull over, throw open the door, and say, "Hop in, buddy." And I won't stop the car too late, so that I bump the guy and send him sliding on his back in the gravel and then he angrily runs up and grabs onto my rear bumper as I try to get away, and I have to fishtail back and forth to shake him off. That day is not quite here, but it's coming.

The Respect of the Men

As leader of the expedition, I have come to realize that there is one thing more important than any other—and that is the respect of the men. It is more valuable than your gun, or your knife, or the blue terry-cloth slippers that keep your feet so toasty around the campfire at night.

In fact, the respect of the men can be even more important than the success of the mission itself. So if you're not exactly sure what the mission is, you may not want to ask the men, because you might lose their respect.

You don't get the respect of the men right away. You can try, by getting down in the dirt and begging them for it, or by kissing their boots, or by doing your funny cowboy dance for them. But trust me, these are not going to work.

No, respect is something that has to be earned. And

earned slowly, like a fine, respectful wine. You can't try to earn it all at once, maybe by doing something like yelling out, "Hey, watch this!" and then rolling all the way down the side of a hill. Even if you explain to the men that there could have been snakes and bees where you rolled, but you didn't care, it won't impress them.

Rather, respect is earned by little things. Let's say you are leading the expedition through the bush, and you announce "I can't go on any farther!" But you do, for about five more hours, until you fall exhausted in the sand. Then you get up and make the men a nice dinner. Things like that.

Or later that night, around the campfire, you are toasting one of your marshmallows, using a stick that you broke off a tree with your bare hands. The marshmallow catches fire, and you wave it around to put it out. Even though it is out, the marshmallow is still smoky-hot and sparky. But you just pop it straight into your mouth.

Or let's say you are riding your horse over some sharp rocks, so you get off to walk your horse, even though the rocks are really rough on your terry-cloth slippers. The men notice things like that. "You're gonna tear up those house shoes," one of the men might say to you. "I know," you mumble, because your mouth is still sore from the burning marshmallow.

That night you might check outside your tent to see if there is a present from the men, which, if you opened it, would be a new pair of slippers. But there isn't. And you smile to yourself, because you realize that the respect of the men is not the same as the love of the men.

But if it is difficult to gain the men's respect, it is easy to lose it. And the worst part is, you don't even know what it was you did. Was it trying to mash nine burning marshmallows into your mouth at once? Was it telling the men that you laugh at danger, but then you don't see any danger so instead you laugh at mountains and trees and horse manure? And Curtis's hat? Was it asking them about the hideous howls during the night that sounded like the lost souls of Hades shrieking in agony and torment, and the men not knowing what you're talking about, then having one of the men say, "Maybe it was a tree frog"?

You can never know for sure. But one thing is certain: You can't win back their respect with cheap parlor tricks or, say, a magic trick. Even if you take hours to learn the trick, and you gather the men around the campfire to perform it, and you use a little magic table that you made yourself, and even if you think the trick is performed pretty well, this is not going to rekindle the men's respect. You can tell from the looks they give one another, and the lack of applause. You may get a little respect if you get mad and throw the table and the trick parts into the fire, but that's about it. And you may get some respect from the dove for letting him go.

But still you are wondering, *What's wrong with these men? Come on, that was a good trick.*

The respect of the men can be a cruel mistress and a harlot. But at other times it can be a nice mistress and a happy slut. You can't think about it too much. But if you ignore it, it can sneak up and coldcock you, like an angry prostitute.

You know it won't be easy, but one day you will again have the respect of the men. You don't know when or how. And you can't help thinking that maybe if you could explain to the men just how difficult the magic trick was, it would go a long way toward getting the whole respect thing going again.

More Favorite Deep Thoughts

Laurie got offended that I used the word "puke." But to me, that's what her dinner tasted like.

If a kid asks where rain comes from, I think a cute thing to tell him is "God is crying." And if he asks why God is crying, another cute thing to tell him is "Probably because of something you did."

There's a world we know nothing about, that we can only imagine. And that is the world of books.

> Blow ye winds,
> Like the trumpet blows;
> But without that noise.

· · · ·

As I bit into the nectarine, it had a crispy juiciness about it that was very pleasurable—until I realized it wasn't a nectarine at all, but a HUMAN HEAD !!

If you ever reach total enlightenment while you're drinking a beer, I bet it makes beer shoot out your nose.

The wise man can pick up a grain of sand and envision a whole universe. But the stupid man will just lay down on some seaweed and roll around until he's completely draped in it. Then he'll stand up and go, "Hey, I'm Vine Man."

There is probably one question that drives just about every vampire crazy: "Oh, do you know Dracula?"

If you're an ant, and you're walking across the top of a cup of pudding, you probably have no idea that the only thing between you and disaster is the strength of that pudding skin.

If you define cowardice as running away at the first sign of danger, screaming and tripping and begging for mercy, then yes, Mister Brave Man, I guess I am a coward.

. . . .

Children need encouragement. So if a kid gets an answer right, tell him it was a lucky guess. That way, he develops a good, lucky feeling.

You know what would make a good story? Something about a clown who makes people happy, but inside he's real sad. Also, he has severe diarrhea.

The Draculas

I knew the Draculas. They called themselves Count Dracula and the Bride of Dracula, but I just called them the Draculas. "Well, if it isn't the Draculas," I'd say.

I met them when I moved in next door. You can get these great old country houses for next to nothing now in Romania. Some families have lived in these houses for hundreds of years, but now they can't pay the taxes, so you can scoop up some great deals.

The Draculas, I have to tell you, were weird. For one thing, all they seemed interested in was blood. I'm not kidding. Blood. That's all they wanted to talk about. If you talked about something else, you could see their eyes sort of glaze over. Every once in a while, I'd drop the word "blood" randomly into the conversation, just to keep it going.

Once, as a gag, I came running out of the kitchen

with ketchup smeared on my hand. "I cut myself!" I yelled. I don't think they thought it was very funny. But how was I to know that Mrs. Dracula would actually lick my hand? Or that she was allergic to ketchup? Man, her face really swelled up. Her teeth look funny anyway, but the swelling made her look extra funny.

The Draculas were also weird about bats, the flying kind. We'd be out back, having martinis at sunset, and the bats would start flying around. I'd light up a Roman candle and fire it at the bats, you know, for fun. I never hit any (except for that one). But I had to stop, because the Draculas would get all upset.

The problem with the Draculas was, they didn't know how to relax. I'd try to get them to play croquet. But when you'd hand them the wooden stake, they'd act like it had cooties or something. Count Dracula would be gingerly tapping it into the ground, and I'd have to go over with my mallet and whack it hard two or three times. "Like that!" I'd say.

Even though the Draculas dressed sexily, I don't think they had much interest in sex. I myself have performed in a couple of adult films, and I offered to loan them copies, but they declined. You'd ask them what good adult films they'd seen lately, but they'd just sort of stammer and change the subject.

I think part of the problem was they were just plain unhealthy. They looked pale and drawn all the time.

Maybe it was from sleeping all day and being up all night. I'd go over to their place in the morning and pound and pound on their big wooden door. Sometimes I'd pound for hours. When I'd see the Draculas again they'd seem annoyed and ask if that was me pounding. Of course it was me! Who else would it be?

So, yes, they were creepy. But I kind of liked them. That's why it was so tragic what happened to them: they moved away.

It all started with my big Fourth of July party. I had invited the Draculas, but they said they couldn't come because they were going to a Fourth of July party at Petru Cozma's house. Which was weird, because Petru Cozma was coming to my party.

Long story short, a couple of big skyrockets from my party got away from me and slammed into the Draculas' place. It started a fire, the fire trucks came, the whole works. I guess all the fire attracted some bats, because a couple of them flew over and got knocked out of the air by the force of a fire hose. I gave the fireman a thumbs-up, because I know how hard it is to hit a bat with a projectile.

I went over, because I like to watch fires, and standing off to one side were the Draculas, soaking wet. "Hey, Draculas," I said. They seemed sad. They said several old paintings and tapestries had burned up. "At least they were old," I said. I asked if they had insurance, but they seemed confused. "What you need," I advised, "is one of those policies with a personal-effects rider."

I would have liked to have stayed, because the fire went on for quite a while, but I had to get back to my party. A few days later I heard the Draculas had left, in the middle of the night. Just pulled out, without even saying good-bye. Like I said, weird. But here's another weird thing. Lately I've had this strange craving. For ketchup. That's right, ketchup. I've started using it on different foods. I had forgotten how much I like it. So, if I ever hear from the Draculas, I'll have to thank them.

Stunned

As I looked through the telescope, I could hardly believe my eyes: There before me, in the constellation of Virgo, circling a medium-sized star, was a planet. And not just any planet. It had oceans and landmasses and polar ice caps, just like Earth.

And then it hit me: Not only was this planet a lot like Earth—it was *exactly* like Earth! It was an exact twin of our very own planet!

I was stunned. I had to walk away from the telescope. An exact copy of Earth! Were there people there? Were they like us? Did they have the same problems, the same hopes? When I finally summoned the courage to look again, I realized that I had been wrong. It wasn't exactly like Earth. The continents didn't have anywhere near the same shapes as ours, the oceans were different, and many other features were dissimilar. Still, it was a planet, and the first conclusive evidence of such outside our own solar system.

Then it hit me: According to my calculations, the entire planet—oceans, continents, and all—was only a mile in diameter, and rotating at more than twenty times per second. It was a world in miniature, spinning at a phenomenal rate of speed!

I was stunned. I sat back in my chair and rubbed my face in bewildered disbelief. After rechecking my calculations, I realized that I had been off on the size of the planet. It wasn't a miniature planet but was instead about the size of our own Earth. And it wasn't spinning as fast as I had originally calculated. In fact, it was spinning much slower—a little bit slower than our own planet. But that didn't dampen my enthusiasm.

What would I call this new planet? It had large blue oceans, continental landmasses, and polar ice caps, not unlike Earth. Then it hit me: this wasn't an exact duplicate of Earth but was very, very similar to an upside-down Earth!

I had to step back from the telescope and steady myself. I looked again, and it still looked like an upside-down Earth, but not as much as it had before. In fact, the more I looked at it, the clearer it became: my God, it wasn't an upside-down Earth likeness at all but an exact duplicate of Earth! I had been right in the first place!

I was stunned. But then I was struck by a thought that was even more devastating: What if it wasn't an exact copy of us but instead we were an exact copy of *it*? The possibilities were fantastic! What were we like, I wondered. Were we warlike? Did we look like humans?

So it was with great disappointment that I realized I had been aiming the telescope at a picture of Earth on the wall. I had been right after all: it *was* a duplicate of Earth. And yet it wasn't a planet. I sat back in my chair, stunned.

When I finally recovered, I began to scan the nighttime skies. What would I find? The possibilities were enormous—everything from an exact duplicate of Earth to a planet that, if you blurred your vision, might look quite similar to our own.

Then I saw it: if that wasn't a hologram of Earth, I don't know what was. But who could be projecting such a hologram? Were they like us? Did they have the same hopes and dreams and hologram projectors? Just as I was being stunned by all of this, I heard a voice: "Wake up, wake up!"

I woke up, and then it hit me: it had all been a dream. I had fallen asleep at the telescope. Then I went back to sleep for about three hours, and this time I didn't dream at all. But I woke up again, and I realized that the next-to-last nap had all been a dream. I was stunned.

"Hey, Bob," I said. "You wouldn't believe the dream I had two naps ago. I dreamed I discovered a planet that was just like our planet, Earth."

"Earth?" said Bob. "Our planet isn't called Earth. It's called Megatron."

I was stunned. What in the name of a supreme being exactly like God was going on here?

"No, wait—I was thinking of another planet," Bob said. "This *is* Earth."

Eagerly, I turned the telescope toward the sky. What new marvels were awaiting me up there? I wondered.

List of Things to Do Today

—Wake up.

—Yawn.

—Untangle self from sheets.

—Brush teeth. If cannot find toothbrush, use toothpaste on finger. If cannot find toothpaste, just rinse mouth with water. (Find glass first.)

—Read newspaper, shake head in disgust. Eat cereal, shake head at how good it is.

—Call work. Find out if I'm still fired.

—Take shower. Get clean, but not so clean it's like you're bragging.

—Fix hammock. Or just lie in it like it is.

—Put lids back on things from previous night.

—Look for ants. Write down number of ants seen. Compare with yesterday's ant list. Note upward or downward trend on ant graph.

—Write chapter of novel. Have Doctor Ponzari trick
  Lance into going into room with moving wall of
  spikes, again.

—Put on pants.

—Change lightbulb. Get neighbors to help, if necessary.

—Put on fake mustache, walk around block. Take off
  mustache, walk around again; look for surprised
  looks on faces.

—Go to drugstore, pick up Viagra. Don't tell phar-
  macist what it's for.

—Buy bag of candy, in case people don't give me
  candy when I go trick-or-treating.

—Ask Old Mister Barnslow where he got the name
  Old Mister Barnslow, and why nobody else calls
  him that.

—Try not to trip over "Jack's Rock." Ignore people
  gathered there to see if I do.

—Watch for skunks, write down number seen. If
  zero again, rethink whole idea of skunk graph.

—Walk to pier, go fishing. If I catch a fish, name him
  Rudy and release him. If no fish, shake fist at water
  and yell, "Well, you win this round, Rudy!"

—Throw rocks at mounds of garbage floating by.
  Make sure not kayakers.

—Ask out girl from payroll department at old job.
  Don't tell her you've been fired.

—Practice funny cowboy dance for at least two hours.
  Concentrate on spinning movements.

—Call Wild Bob and ask him if he's gotten over his no-drinking phase yet.

—Have staring contest with cat. Then go buy cat toys, like I do every day.

—Learn karate, from book I bought. Pick fight with big guy next door.

—Refill bird feeder; use bird seed this time.

—Call around, see if I am in anyone's will.

—Work on design for the Everyday Helmet. Should be thick enough to protect head after tripping, and to repel objects thrown at head, but light enough to be casual.

—Meditate for an hour, lying down, on the couch.

—Fight inner demon. Let inner demon win so he doesn't feel bad.

—Call up Don, see if I can borrow some more money. Remind Don I have finished making Voodoo Don.

—Do something just for fun. Go fly a kite. Or go to a bar and get really drunk, and complain about the government.

—Ask person on street for the time. Check my watch to see if he's lying. Nod and say "You passed" if time is the same. Just shake head and walk away if not.

—Practice head shaking.

—Lie in hammock, count shooting stars. See if number continues to have eerie similarity to number of ants. Nobel Prize?

—Get out telescope. Check on college girls, to make sure they're okay.

—Thank the man upstairs for putting a roof over your head. On second thought, don't thank him, as he may raise rent.

—Prepare next day's list of things to do. If too tired, just use this one again.

—Make self big martini. You deserve it!

—Have sweet dreams.

The Greatest Fly Fisherman I Ever Knew

The greatest fly fisherman I ever knew was a big bear of a man. When he stood up straight, he was well over six feet tall. He had powerful, hairy arms and massive, hair-covered legs. His body was also hairy. For some reason, he kept his fingernails and toenails long and sharp. He didn't need a lot of fancy equipment to catch fish. In fact, most of the time he didn't even use a rod and reel. He would just wade out in the river, reach down, and catch a fish with his bare hands. Sometimes he'd just stick his head underwater and catch one with his teeth!

He didn't believe in highfalutin, "politically correct" ideas like catch and release. Whatever he caught, he ate—usually right there, while it was still alive. Once I even saw him eat a muskrat. The only thing he liked better than fish was honey. He'd sniff out a beehive and tear it open with those long fingernails of his.

Sometimes the bees would sting him and he'd let out a big roar of pain. I'd usually start laughing and he'd charge over and swat me across the head, opening up my scalp. But it was all in good fun. I think the only other thing I ever saw him eat was garbage.

He didn't say much. In fact, hardly anything. He'd puff and growl if he didn't like the story you were telling, and you'd usually have to play dead until he calmed down. But then, after another bowl of whiskey, he'd be ready for the rest of the story.

He seemed to follow his own set of rules. For instance, he never wore any clothes. And trust me, he didn't like you trying to put clothes on him. Another one of his quirks was, well, he stank. He never bathed and his breath was terrible. Even after you offered him a mint, and he took the whole roll away from you and ate it, his breath was still bad. At least when he would defecate, he'd go in the woods.

Even worse, he had a drug problem. More than once I saw him staggering around, disoriented, with a syringe stuck in his buttock. The authorities would come and carry him away, usually in a net hanging underneath a helicopter. But a few days later he'd be right back, raring to fish.

And boy, could he fish! In fact, when other fishermen saw him coming, they'd usually run away, screaming, because they knew they wouldn't be catching anything while he was around.

After the fishing season ended, he seemed to lose interest in just about everything but sleeping. I think he'd sleep right through the winter if I let him, which I finally learned to do, after repeated skull bites.

People ask what was the most important thing I learned from him about fishing. I guess it would be that you don't need to be a slave to matching the hatch. A lot of times you'll get just as many fish by chasing them into shallow water and pouncing on them. Or by stealing them from other fishermen.

The odd thing is, I never knew his name. Some people would yell out "Griz!" when they saw him, but I don't think that was it. I tried calling him "Lonnie" for a while, but that didn't seem to stick either. When I think back on it, all I can do is scratch my head, and then wince, from the stitches in my scalp.

But this spring I discovered the most surprising thing of all, when I saw him again after the long off-season. With him were two of the cutest, hairiest little children I had ever seen. And then it finally hit me: the greatest fly fisherman I ever knew wasn't a man at all, but a woman.

Waffle and Pancake Council

As new president of the Waffle and Pancake Council, I am pleased to announce that the council has returned to its old mission of promoting waffles and pancakes. The crime phase is over. The ringleader, Doctor Ponzari (real name Willard Cadwallader) has been kicked upstairs, along with his chief henchman, Extractus. Others have been demoted or offered early retirement.

I wish to apologize to all those we killed or addicted to drugs. This was certainly not the goal of our founder, Abraham Cadwallader, when he started the Waffle and Pancake Council in 1905.

We knew we had to act when, as recently as two years ago, public opinion surveys showed that the things most associated with the council were "baby-stealing," "extortion," and "running over people with a motorboat." "Waffles" and "pancakes" were not even in the top ten.

Things first started to go bad, in my view, in 1962. That's when the council announced that it would promote not only waffles and pancakes, but also, where appropriate, bank robbery. At first we targeted banks that did not hold at least one annual pancake breakfast. But soon even that restriction was dropped.

The council was involved in everything from arson and prostitution to giving away waffle irons that we knew would break after just a few uses. The low point probably came in 1973, when the council announced that waffles and pancakes "suck."

There was a brief period of reform in which the council went back to promoting pancakes, but only ones laced with psychotropic drugs, to turn people into mindless killing machines. The quality of the free waffle irons was much improved, but only because they were used to imprint crime instructions in the waffles.

Things reached a crisis point in 2005 when the Waffle and Pancake Council announced that it had acquired nuclear weapons. The device itself was nothing more than a flat cake of plutonium which, when struck with a uranium spatula by an unknowing stooge, was supposed to explode. The press had a field day. And even though most scientists agreed that the bomb would not have worked, it was enough to give pause to some on the council.

Across the country, local waffle council presidents spoke up, and were assassinated. But the message was starting to get through. The Cadwallader family received thousands of letters from ordinary citizens telling how they had been kidnapped and tortured by the council, or had been promised money for delivering drugs but still had not received payment.

That's when I was brought in. After the personnel shakeup, the first thing I did was fire the advertising agency that produced the spots which had hypnotized so many people. Next, I ordered that the council by-laws be rewritten so that the definitions of "pancake" and "waffle" were more traditional, and not so vague that "pancake" could mean practically anything.

Doctor Ponzari's hideaway, Skull Island, is being restored to its original shape and topography, and has been given its old name, Turtle Head Island. Also, the inhabitants of the island have been set free and given electric mixers, without charge.

Safeguards have been set up. All council members must have picture IDs, and if your face is surgically altered to hide your identity, you must get a *new* picture ID. Eye patches are prohibited, even with a note from a doctor. The council will promote waffles and pancakes only as food items, and not as "high-speed projectiles" or "suffocating devices." We are also severing

ties with our so-called "sister council," the Muffin &
Dynamite Board.

The council chamber has been renovated. The dramatic under lighting, which made everyone look so
sinister, has been taken out. The microphone system
has been adjusted back to normal, so people's voices
don't have that ominous bass sound. The chamber is
now no-smoking.

I don't kid myself. It will take years to get things
completely back to normal. For instance, in a conces-
sion to some senior council members, it was agreed
that we would not only promote waffles and pancakes
but also a type of maple syrup whose fumes, when re-
leased, will knock you out. Doctor Ponzari is still technically chairman of the board, but his deranged
memos are now quietly filed away.

In short, we are back to pushing buckwheat, not
buckshot. We sing the praises of the Belgian waffle,
and not the "Mexican Waffle," which is a type of torture. I am hopeful that the words of Abraham Cadwallader, carved in wood and now back on the wall
where the missile-tracking screen used to be, will once
again guide us: "All a boy needs to keep himself
amused is a good pancake."

Some Funny
New York Things

The other day I was thinking up some funny New York things, and here are some of the things I came up with:

A guy is in the subway, and suddenly he turns into a monster. I don't know why he does, and it doesn't really matter. But here's the funny part: another guy comes up to him and asks him what time it is, and it doesn't even bother him that the guy is a monster! Can you believe it?!

Or how about this: there's a long line of people waiting to pay for their groceries, and some lady comes and tries to cut in line, and the other people just yell at her! I don't believe it! They don't even know her, but they yell at her anyway!

But you can't talk about New York unless you talk about the subway. Oh, wait, I already did that one.

What about how expensive the apartments are. Picture this in your mind: a pirate is trying to rent an apartment, and he has his treasure chest with him, and he asks the landlord how much of his treasure will he have to use to pay for the rent. And the landlord says, "All of it." All of it?! Now, that's a high rent!

And what about the cabs, you're saying. I was just getting to that. But first I have an idea for a situation comedy that I want to put in here. Maybe it could be in New York, I don't know. Anyway, a funny situation comedy would be one where Dick Butkus is married to Zsa Zsa Gabor, because think of it: Dick Butkus and Zsa Zsa Gabor! They're not even alike, those two!

First, Dick Butkus comes home. Then he starts yelling, "Zsa Zsa, I'm home!" At first you don't see Zsa Zsa, and you're thinking, Oh, no, what has Zsa Zsa gotten herself into now?!

But then she finally comes out, and she's holding a gun. "I'm going to kill you, Dick Butkus," she says, "because we're not alike at all. I'm Zsa Zsa Gabor, and you're a big football player."

I don't know what happens next, but so far it's pretty good, don't you think?

Oh, anyway, the thing I was saying about New York cabs is, the drivers are all from foreign countries. I'm not sure why that's funny, but it seems like it is. Maybe what's funny is there's a cab driver who's real goofy and funny, and he drives so wild that you fall out of the cab onto the street! Hey, come back here!

And even though you're all scraped up and your bones are broken, a wino comes up to you and says, "Gimme some money." Gimme some money?! Your bones are all broken, but he still says gimme some money! He's a New York wino, all right!

I can't think of any more funny New York things right now. So *EXCUUUUSE ME*!

Little Tiny Stories

Slim Pickings

I had never eaten dog before, and I didn't intend to start now. "Just give me some more of the copilot," I said, extending my plate.

Blow Dart

The first blow dart hit me in the neck. The second hit me in the leg. After that, I blacked out. When I woke up, I asked Lelani how many blow darts had hit me. She seemed annoyed. "What am I," she said, "your personal blow dart counter?"

Invisible Guy

If it worked correctly, the paste I was smearing on my body would make me invisible. And even if it didn't, it would probably moisturize my skin.

LOST WORLD

A world ruled by dinosaurs? It didn't make any sense! I could understand a world where dinosaurs had some say, but not rule.

DRUGGED

After I finished my second double gin and tonic, I felt woozy, unstable on my feet. Then I realized: my drink had probably been drugged! I had a beer, then two more, to clean out my system, but they made me feel even dizzier. I thought some exercise might counteract the drug, so I got up on the diving board and started dancing. But it was no use. When the drug finally wore off, I was lying in the backyard wearing nothing but a hula skirt.

THE CURSE FULFILLED

As I watched in horror, Lucinda's face grew old, hideously old, right before my eyes! The curse had come true! Hoping she didn't notice, I slipped her engagement ring back into my coat pocket.

A HARSH LESSON

I tried to explain to little Betsy how, when horses get old, you have to take them out and shoot them. But then I thought, Why not wait until she gets a horse?

THE SEVERED HEAD

You don't forget the first time you ever see a severed head. Especially if it's your best friend, Don. And especially if he's got a cigar clenched between his teeth, even though the last time you saw your so-called friend he swore he didn't have any more cigars.

GENETIC EXPERIMENTS

While I was looking around the nursery, I suddenly realized: these weren't ordinary children; these were children specially bred by Doctor Ponzari and his wife to be their own family!

ADRIFT

I drifted in the lifeboat for days, maybe months. To be honest, I guess it wasn't months. That would be too long. "Weeks" is probably too long too, because I would have dried out or something by then. "Hours" is too short. To tell you the truth, I don't even think it was a lifeboat.

BIG SHOES AND BULLETS

I knew if I was ever going to catch the killer clown, it wasn't going to be enough to dress up like a clown. I also had to *think* like a clown.

THE LOOK ON HER FACE

"Hold on to my hand!" I yelled.

"I can't!" said Lucinda. "I'm slipping!"

"Hold on!" I screamed. But it was too late. She let go, and fell, landing hard on her buttocks. And that was the last time we ever went square-dancing.

A Grim Discovery

When I looked into the microscope, I couldn't believe my eyes. The deadly dangerous germs I had been studying were now dead. All dead! Now, how was I going to study them and find a cure for them? Whoever or whatever had killed them was going to be in big trouble.

The Choice

I picked up a stick and drew a line in the sand. "Whoever wants to go with me, cross over on this side," I said. Tears welled up in my eyes. Before I even finished speaking, all three of my dogs crossed over. Then Scruffy grabbed the stick and ran away with it.

Native Lore

So this was what the natives called the "terror bird." It turned out to be nothing more than a gigantic forty-foot eagle that shot fire out of its mouth.

The Lurker Below

As I maneuvered the one-man sub into the enemy harbor, I smiled a little smile to myself. It amused me to

think that the people of Massachusetts did not even realize that a Connecticut resident was right under their
very noses.

THE SAD FAREWELL
I tried to explain to Lelani that she could not come
back with me to civilization, that she would die there.
A tear trickled down her cheek. Then she put something in my hand.

It was a shrunken head—the same one that had
made us laugh so much that first day.

MARTIAN TRICKERY
The Martians hooked me up to what I thought was a
lie detector, but turned out to be a torture device. And
after that, they had me sign what I thought was a
recording contract, but which turned out to be a confession.

PREY, TELL ME
As I understood it, the tribe would give me a head
start, and then they would hunt me down, for sport. I
got an idea. Instead of running, I began to ask them a
bunch of questions about the rules, to stall and confuse
them. That's when the clubbing began.

My First Day in Hell

My first day in Hell is drawing to a close. They don't really have a sunset here, but the fires seem to dim a bit, and the screaming gets more subdued. Many of the demons are asleep now, their pointy tails curled up around themselves. They look so innocent, it's hard to believe that just a few hours ago they were raping and torturing us.

The day started off at a party at the Chelsea Hotel, where some friends were daring me to do something. The next thing I knew, I was in Hell. At first it seemed like a dream, but then you remember that five-martini dreams are usually a lot worse.

The ferry boat across the River Styx was so overcrowded, I thought the whole thing was going to tip over. In fact, some demons onboard were trying to rock us back and forth. Still, the sight of the towering cliffs of Hell, with evil, grinning dolphins swimming alongside, is an unforgettable one. "Wow, is this really Hell?" I said to the guy next to me. He said yeah, it was. I asked him again, to make sure, but that made him start crying. Man, what's with that guy?

There's a kind of customs station, where a skeleton in a black robe checks a big book to make sure you're in there. It's kind of boring, but I guess you have to do it. As his bony finger slowly scans the pages, searching for your name, you can't help thinking, What does a skeleton need with a robe? Especially since it's so hot. That's the first thing you notice about Hell, how hot it is. I'm not going to lie to you, it's *hot*. But it's a steamy, sulfur kind of hot. Like a spa or something.

You might think people in Hell are all nude. But that's a myth. You wear what you were last wearing. For instance, I am dressed like the German U-boat captain in the movie *Das Boot,* because that's what I wore to the party. It's an easy costume, because all you really need is the hat. The bad part is people are always asking you who you are, even in Hell. Come on, I'm the guy from *Das Boot!*

The food here turns out to be surprisingly good. The trouble is, just about all of it is poisoned. So a few minutes after eating you're doubled over in agony. The weird thing is, after you recover, you're ready to dig in all over again.

Despite the tasty food and warm weather, there's a dark side to Hell. For one thing, it's totally disorganized.

How anything gets done down here is a miracle. You'll be herded along in one big line, then it'll separate into three lines, then they'll all come back together again! For no apparent reason! It's crazy. You try to ask a demon a question, but he just looks at you. I don't mean to sound prejudiced, but you wonder if they even speak English.

To relieve the boredom, you can throw rocks at other people in line. They'll just think it was a demon or something. But I discovered the hard way that the demons don't like it when they're beating someone and you join in.

It's odd, but Hell can be a lonely place, even with so many people. They all seem caught up in their own little worlds, running to and fro, wailing and tearing at their hair. You try to make conversation, but you can tell they're not listening.

A malaise sets in. I thought getting a job might help. It turns out I have a lot of relatives in Hell, and using connections, I became assistant to a demon who pulls people's teeth out. It wasn't actually a job, more of an internship. But I was eager. And at first it was kind of interesting. But after a while you start asking yourself: Is this what I came to Hell for, to hand different kinds of pliers to a demon? I started wondering if I even should have come to Hell at all. Maybe I should have lived my life differently and gone to Heaven instead. I was tormented.

I had to get away. The endless lines, the senseless whipping, the forced sing-alongs. You get tired of trying to explain that you've already been branded, or that something that big won't fit in your ear, even with a hammer. I wandered off. I needed some "me" time. I came to a cave and went inside. Maybe I would find a place to meditate, or some gold nuggets.

That's when it happened, one of those moments that could happen only in Hell. I saw Satan. Some people have been in Hell for thousands of years and have never seen Satan, but there he was. He was shorter than I expected, and wearing a baseball cap. But he looked pretty good. He was standing on top of a big rock, looking at some papers with his reading glasses. I think he was practicing a speech or something. "Hey, Satan," I yelled out, "how's it going?" I was immediately set upon by demons. I can't begin to describe the tortures they inflicted on me, because apparently they are trade secrets. Suffice it to say that, even as you endure all the pain, you find yourself thinking, Wow, how did they think of *that*?

I'm still feeling a little dizzy, but at least the demons stuffed most of my parts back in me. But, more important, my faith in Hell as an exciting place where anything could happen has been restored. Hell, I've found, is what you make of it.

I had better get some rest. They say the bees will be out soon, and that it's hard to sleep with the constant stinging. I lost my internship, but apparently I can reapply in one hundred years. Meanwhile, I've been assigned to a construction crew. Tomorrow we're supposed to build a huge monolith, then take picks and shovels and tear it down, then beat each other to death. It sounds pointless to me, but what do I know? I'm new here.

Animals All Around Us

Most people don't realize there is an unseen, mysterious world all around us. No, I'm not talking about the world of invisible scary monsters. I am talking about the world of bizarre little animals that live alongside us right in our homes. They inhabit our clothing, our furniture, our piles of old rags, our pans of dripping rainwater—even our bodies themselves.

Some of these creatures are so microscopic you can barely even see them. Others are bigger, but you probably can't see them without your glasses, if you wear them.

We usually don't even notice these animals, but they're there. Take, for instance, the little creatures that are constantly flying around our heads all day. These, it turns out, are houseflies. They can live off the scraps of food that fall from our mouths while chewing. And they are able to reproduce right in the house, in dog droppings.

Or consider even smaller animals, which live unnoticed among the hairs of our private regions. They are called crabs. No, don't worry, they aren't actual crabs. And they certainly aren't large enough to eat, unless you could somehow get thousands of them. But they are with us, year after year.

Have you ever noticed how old chili beans and ground-up pieces of potato chips will magically seem to move around on the living room carpet? This is actually caused by ants. Ants? But don't they live in caves or something? That's what I used to think. But if you look closely, you can see them almost everywhere.

Some animals are masters of disguise. What you may think are raisins, stuck to your legs after hours of lying on the couch, are often what scientists call leeches. Where do they come from? Where *don't* they come from is more like it. But most often we pick them up wading through the basement.

There are even organisms that manage to get into our appliances and live there undisturbed. These are rats. Many times the only clue to their presence is a zapping noise, some smoke, and a smell that can linger for weeks.

Incredibly, some little animals are able to infiltrate the very liquids we drink. They are called yeast, and we consume them by the billions, hour after hour, every day.

Other creatures are larger, but elusive. When you get up in the middle of the night for more bites of the chicken piece you left on the counter, you may have to fight for it with a raccoon. One reason we rarely notice these furry interlopers is they come and go through holes in the wall. Also, a lot of times when we fight them we're drunk, and later we think we imagined it.

You might suppose that at least when you climb into bed you would be free of the animal kingdom. But suppose again. There, too, they are watching us, crawling on us, waiting for the opportunity to bite. These are our cats, swarming over us throughout the night.

No doubt some of these invaders can be harmful. One animal can literally eat its way through the wood that holds the house together. This is the common beaver. He is attracted to the water overflowing from our basements, which he tries to dam up. Another harmful pest is the moth, which can fly in your mouth when you're taking a nap.

But many of the creatures living in our homes can be beneficial. Take drifters, for example. Sometimes they will go to the store to get you things (although they usually "lose" the change). Termites will often leave piles of sawdust around, which can be used to soak up stains. And mice entertain us by playing musical instruments. No, wait, I'm thinking of cartoon mice.

Through millions of years of evolution, animals have adapted to thrive in every corner of our world, from our empty Cup-a-Soup containers to the dried-up branches and dusty ornaments of our Christmas trees. They inhabit the bristles of our toothbrushes, the bristles of our whiskers, and the bristles of our cheese.

The temptation is to want to do something about them. But what? You can throw cats off the bed, but they just jump right back on. Virtually every kind of alcoholic beverage has yeast swimming in it. You can scrub the crabs off your body, but what are you going to do about your bedsheets, or your sweatpants? Wash *them* too? You could drive yourself crazy.

Even if we could get rid of all these animals with a magic wand, would we want to? Yes, of course we would—why would you even ask that? But maybe the best answer, as with most things, is just to do nothing at all.

However, that's not what the health department thinks. They have hit me with a large fine and ordered me to "clean up" my property. But ultimately we have to ask ourselves: Do we want to live in some soulless antiseptic world ruled by futuristic robots, where dishes are cleaned every day and sinks and toilets are an eerie, gleaming white? I don't think that we do. I think people would rather live in homes where animals roam wild and free, in our hair, in our bags of things, and in our underpants.

Glug-Glug-Glug

The glug-glug-glug symbol is one of the most time-honored of all the human hand gestures. This is the sign you use when you want to indicate—often behind someone's back—that he has been drinking. Usually, your clenched fingers form a "bottle," and your extended thumb a spout. Then you hold the "bottle" up and "drink." You can make a glug-glug-glug sound if you want to. It's up to you.

Scientists say glug-glug-glug is preceded in evolution only by the "over there" point and the "pee-yew" nose squeeze. Glug-glug-glug has been used throughout history. It is said that when Patrick Henry declared, "Give me liberty or give me death!" half the people behind him did the glug-glug-glug sign. When Abraham Lincoln was shot, the first usher to reach him mistakenly did the glug-glug-glug sign. During the 1960s, people experimented with new gestures, and glug-glug-glug was replaced by the "toke" symbol. But today glug-glug-glug is stronger than ever.

All I know is glug-glug-glug broke my heart.

It started when I went to try to get a job with my uncle Lou. I thought he could make me a vice president in his company. I had had trouble reaching him by phone, so I just showed up at his office. His secretary, Shirley, tried to keep me waiting, but I just barged right in. "Hey, Uncle Lou!" I shouted. But he was gone. I looked out through the open window, and shimmying down the trellis was Uncle Lou. Shirley and I looked at each other and, together, did the glug-glug-glug sign.

We started dating. We did glug-glug-glug everywhere. If we went to the ballet, and the male dancer did a perfect pirouette, we did glug-glug-glug. If he slipped slightly, we also did glug-glug-glug. It didn't matter. It worked either way.

Of course, when Shirley and I got married and the preacher said "till death do you part," we did a little subtle glug. Looking back, maybe we should have taken the whole thing more seriously.

Glug-glug-glug got old. Shirley and I realized that we had little in common, and that we didn't even like each other. One night I came home with lipstick on my collar. When Shirley asked about it, all I could do was the index-finger-through-the-circled-fingers sign.

We tried counseling, but it was hopeless. In our last

session, when the counselor suddenly got up and said, "I've got to go do something, *right now,*" we didn't even look at each other, let alone do glug-glug-glug.

When I read the divorce papers, I did the blowing-out-my-brains sign. For a long time, friends would come by and do the let's-go-fishing sign or the let's-go-to-a-museum sign (where you put your hand to your chin and act like you're looking at a painting). But I would just do the I'm-taking-a-nap sign.

Finally, I went to a friend's party. Someone was up on a table, doing a funny cowboy dance. Even though the dance was really hilarious, something made me look away. There was Wendy, also laughing. She looked radiant and beautiful. Somehow I caught her eye. We smiled and, instinctively, both did the glug-glug-glug sign. Then I did the how-about-a-drink sign, which is like glug-glug-glug, only your hand is holding a glass instead of a bottle.

When Wendy and I walked home that night, hand in hand, I couldn't help thinking that maybe, just maybe, some things are meant to last. Perhaps in the future, outer-space aliens will land on an Earth devastated by nuclear destruction, turn to one another and make the glug-glug-glug sign.

Fuzzy Memories

I think the best Thanksgiving I ever had was the one where we didn't even have a turkey. Mom and Dad sat us kids down and explained that business hadn't been good at Dad's store, so we couldn't afford a turkey. We had vegetables and bread and pie, and it was just fine.

Later I went into Mom and Dad's bedroom to thank them, and I caught them eating a little turkey.

I guess that wasn't really the *best* Thanksgiving.

When we would go for a drive in the family car, I used to love to stick my head out the window, until one time we passed an oncoming car and my head knocked off a dog's head.

When I was seven, I told my friend Timmy Barker I would give him a million dollars if he would eat an earthworm. He ate the worm, but I never gave him the million dollars. As of last week, all I had given him was $9,840.

One day Dad asked me to go fishing with him. I got scared. I had the feeling he was going to try to drown me. I don't know why I thought that, because so far he had never tried to kill me. But he had never taken me fishing either, so I was suspicious.

When we got to the lake, he walked right up to it. "Hey, son, come here," he said. "Look at these minnows."

"Nice try, Dad—if that's your real name!" I yelled. Then I ran back to the car and locked myself in.

Dad never took me fishing again. So I think that proves my case.

I remember when we were kids, one of our favorite games was to play "pirate." We'd dress up like pirates. Then we'd go find an adult walking down the street and we'd go up to him and pull out our butcher knives, which we called "swords," and say, "We're pirates! Give us your money!" A lot of adults would pretend to be scared and give us their money. Others would suddenly run away, yelling for help. We played pirate until we were twenty or so.

Mom used to make the most beautiful Easter eggs. Then she'd hide them in the backyard. But they were so beautiful, when we found one, we weren't allowed to pick it up. We had to point at it, and then Mom would come pick it up with her white gloves and put it back in its case.

Somebody ended up smashing all those eggs with a hammer. I think it was our dog.

When you're ten years old, and a car drives by and splashes a puddle of water all over you, it's hard to decide if you should go to school like that or try to go home and change and probably be late. So while he was trying to decide, I drove by and splashed him again.

When I was in the third grade, a bully at school started beating me up, every day. At first I didn't say anything, but then I told Dad. He got a real scared look on his face and asked if the bully had a big dad. I said I didn't know, but he still seemed scared, and just a few days later we moved to a new town.

Dad told me if anybody picked on me not to fight back, unless I knew the kid didn't have a dad or the dad was real small. Otherwise, he said, "Just curl up in a ball."

It was really sad when I went to visit my friend Jim at the state mental institution. He was convinced he was on a tropical island with no cares and no worries. It took me a long time to convince him that no, he was in a room with bare walls and a bare bed and he was wearing a straitjacket.

Once, when I got lost in the woods, I was afraid that eventually I might have to eat Tippy. But finally I found my way home, and I was able to put Tippy back in the refrigerator with my other sandwiches.

Mom always told me I could be whatever I wanted to be when I grew up, "within reason." When I asked her what she meant by "within reason," she said, "You ask a lot of questions for a garbage man."

One year Dad decided he was going to take us on a "surprise vacation." We wouldn't know where we were going until we got there. We were all real excited when we piled into the station wagon early one morning. We went about five blocks, then we got in an accident at a four-way stop.

I guess it was a pretty good surprise, but why did we need all that camping gear?

I remember one night I was walking past Mom and Dad's room when I heard them talking about how they might not have enough money to pay their bills that month. I knew what I had to do. I went and got my piggy bank and buried it in the backyard, where they couldn't get their mitts on it.

• • • •

When Dad found out the house was full of termites, he got real mad. But I was glad, because now I wouldn't have to go all the way to the woods to get termites for my termite farm.

When I was about ten years old, we set up a lemonade stand on the sidewalk in front of our house. But we didn't sell many glasses, and after a few hours, we took it down. I think that was the first time I realized that the world doesn't give a damn about you or anything you do.

I'll never forget the time the president came to our town. When I saw him go by, he looked so much older and sadder than I thought he was. Also, why was he driving an ice cream truck?

I remember lying there and watching an anthill for hours. I would watch them scurrying back and forth, carrying things, digging new tunnels, and finally it hit me: these are the things that are biting me.

Of all my imaginary friends, I don't think there was one I didn't end up having to kill.

In Praise of
the Human Body

When you think of the most amazing machine in the world, what do you think of? James Bond's car, right? But recently I had a thought that may surprise you, and even startle you: the most amazing machine in the world is the human body. That's right, the human body.

But how, you say, can the human body be a machine? It doesn't have a central pump, or rotating joints, or interlocking teeth. But think again—doesn't it?

Not only is the human body the greatest machine, but the greatest oil for a machine is any oil that goes on the human body. I'm not sure about sex oils, but Oil of Olay, Pond's Cold Cream, oils such as these are the most beautiful of oils.

The most magnificent warranty on a machine would be some type of warranty on a human body, which I guess would be a life insurance policy, something like that.

The greatest hood ornament for a machine is one of those mirror things a doctor wears on his head.

For me, the greatest work of art in the world is also the human body. I'm not talking about an old body or an ugly one. I mean a really hot, sexy body. Man, to me, that's great art. And the greatest way to view the art is by hiding in the bushes and hoping the art doesn't see you.

The greatest temple in the world is, let's face it, the Parthenon. But if the Parthenon gets any more corroded, I think I'm going to have to say the human body.

What's the most perfect musical instrument? I would argue it's the human body, except for the tuba sounds.

The greatest thing that can be sewn together from different parts and then brought back to life with electricity is the human body.

The most precious gift one human can give another, I believe, is the gift of a third human, such as a prostitute or stripper, for a birthday or something.

The fiercest battleground in the world is the human body. But the battle is fought on a microscopic level, which makes it the most boring battleground.

The best friend you can have is the human body, unless it's dead and it's chasing you.

The greatest envy of the chimpanzee is the human body, especially the roller-skating human body.

The greatest cannibal meal in the world is, surprisingly, strawberry shortcake.

The greatest engineering miracle of all time is, okay, Hoover Dam. But what else can hold back water and release it gradually, to prevent flooding? And what else can generate "electricity," maybe by getting up and doing its funny cowboy dance? Isn't it the human body?

The greatest evidence of a murder is the human body.

The greatest monument to human stupidity is the Washington Monument, if it ever falls over because it wasn't built very good.

The greatest medicine in the world is human laughter. And the worst medicine is zombie laughter.

The greatest mystery in the world is the human heart, but only while it's in the human body. Otherwise, where's the mystery?

The most amazing computer ever made is the human brain. And the best way to shut down the human brain is have it listen to my so-called friend Don.

The greatest camera is the human eye, but a worse camera is the drunk human eye. And a really bad camera is the drunk eye that has been punched by the human fist.

I'm not sure what the greatest weapon in the world is, but one of the worst weapons is one of those bowls in bars that holds peanuts, because when you throw it at a guy it just makes him madder.

In general, though, I would say the human body or its parts or the things that come out of it are the best in their categories. And even after it dies the human body has one more trick up its sleeve: it turns into the scariest skeleton in the world.

Don says the only reason I come up with ideas about the human body is to sound smart at parties. But I don't just toss off ideas haphazardly, like you would toss a horseshoe over your shoulder. I study an idea, then I chew on it for a while, then I spit it out. So, Don, don't think I'm just trying to sound smart, because I'm not.

Attila the Hun's Greatest Speech

(Of what are generally regarded as the "Ten Greatest Speeches of Attila the Hun," the following is perhaps the least known. However, many notable writers and statesmen have borrowed from it throughout the centuries, and it is now generally considered the greatest speech ever given by a Hun.)

Four score and seven weeks ago, we came into this land, killing and raping everything we could get our hands on. And we did a good job. Never in the course of human conflict have so many been trampled so much, with so few regrets.

When we set out, all I could promise you was the blood, sweat, and tears of our victims, and also all their stuff. And I have given you that. I also promised you a rose garden, which I am working on.

Our guiding principle is that a house divided cannot

stand. Neither can a peasant, although it's funny to watch him try. And so we conquer. Our battle cry, "Damn the torpedoes! Full steam ahead!" has confused and frightened our enemies. I'm not sure what it means myself, but it seems to work.

It's been fun to be a Hun. We enjoy life, liberty, and the pursuit of screaming villagers. But maybe you should ask not who the Huns can kill for you, but who you can kill for the Huns.

Some of you may have heard about the bad break I got. Last night I was offered a bowl of dates for dessert. And I ate a date—a date which will live in infamy. It troubled my bowels throughout the night. Believe me, it was not some enchanted evening. Yet today, now that it's over, I consider myself the luckiest man on the face of the earth. And you know who the unluckiest men are? Probably those prisoners over there in that cage. Is it better to suffer the slings and arrows of out-of-practice archers, or to have a hot coal put in your eye? It's hard to say, both hurt a lot.

Finally, we stand at the gates of Rome. All roads, I have learned, lead to Rome. I wish I had known that before. That way, instead of wandering all over the place, we could have just gotten on a road and followed it here. It would have been a lot easier.

I come not to praise Caesar, but to bury him. But he won't let me. He struts around on that rampart, sticking his tongue out at us. Instead he should be rebuking his generals, telling them, "Well, this is another fine mess you've gotten us into."

Caesar, tear down this wall! Or at least open the gates and we'll tear it down for you. And don't delay. As I told the Germans, *Ich bin ein crazy guy*.

Let me conclude by saying, friends, captured Romans, and countrymen, lend me your ears. I'm not kidding. Cut them off and put them in a big pile here. I will use them on my rose garden.

And now, please welcome a time traveler from the future. I hope I am pronouncing his name right: Knute Rockne.

(It is not known what Rockne said, although it is believed he referred to Notre Dame football player George Gipp, and urged the Huns to win one for the Gipper. Rockne's time machine was then torn apart by the Huns and used as fencing for Attila's garden.)

Mount Everest

When I think back on all the times I've climbed Mount Everest, it brings a smile to my leathery, frostbitten face.

The first time I climbed Mount Everest, I was only ten years old. I was lucky to make it to the top. I didn't know what I was doing. I was only wearing corduroys, a Windbreaker, and Keds.

After that, I decided to get some real mountain-climbing gear. I got some boots with those spiky things on the bottom, and I got one of those ice pick things. To be honest, you don't really need the ice pick thing, but it looks cool in photos. You might also want to take some rope; any kind will do.

I have climbed using oxygen and without oxygen. Once I climbed using helium, so my voice would sound funny. When I was younger, I climbed Mount Everest five times in a row. Every time I got to the bottom, I said to myself, "What the heck, I'm going back up."

I guess I must have been getting bored, because about my fifteenth time, when I got to the top, I piled up a bunch of rocks to make Mount Everest a few feet higher, and then stood on that. But the next time I reached the peak, someone had scattered the rocks and left a sign that read, DON'T PILE UP ROCKS. Screw you, I'll pile up rocks if I want to!

Whether it's rude signs or altitude sickness, Everest is always a challenge. It's like a woman. A cold, unapproachable woman that you've made love to dozens of times. But sometimes you are denied. Once I was within a few hundred yards of the summit when I had to turn back. I remembered I had to go to a bachelor party back at base camp, and I would have been late. Another time I made the mistake of starting my climb after dark. Also, I was drunk. I stumbled around all night. Finally, at dawn, I struggled onto the summit. But it turned out to be the wrong mountain!

Probably my most difficult ordeal on Everest was when I attempted to climb it nude. I hadn't started out nude. But it was a nice, warm day, and on my way up, I decided to take off my clothes and catch some rays. A blizzard suddenly moved in, and blew my clothes away.

I had a decision to make: I could turn back, or I could continue on, naked. I decided to go on. The blizzard got worse. I became disoriented. Finally, I spotted a Sherpa's hut and knocked weakly on the door. The Sherpa answered. "Excuse me, sir," I said, "but I'm climbing Everest and I've become nude." I asked if I could spend the night. "You can spend the night," he said, eyeing me suspiciously. "Just don't try any funny business with my daughter." It was then that I noticed a beautiful, buxom girl peeking out from behind him.

To make a long story short, I did make it to the top, wearing a woman's dress and carrying a load of shotgun pellets in my buttocks.

Sometimes I wonder: How many more Everest climbs do I have in me? A hundred? Two hundred? It's hard to say. All I know is that I hope I can keep climbing Everest until the day I die. And even after I die, maybe some type of high-voltage stimulator could be implanted in my brain, so that I sort of flop uphill, spasmodically. That's my dream anyway.

The Voices in My Head

I never know when the voices in my head are going to start talking to me. I might be coming out of my apartment and I'll look up at the clouds. Suddenly, the voices in my head will tell me to go back inside and get an umbrella, because it might rain. Sometimes I'll obey the voices and go get the umbrella. But sometimes I muster my strength and refuse to get the umbrella. Still, the voices don't let you forget that you disobeyed them, especially if it rains. They'll say, "I knew you should have gotten the umbrella. Why didn't you?"

I don't expect you to understand what it's like to have voices in your head telling you what to do. But it is a nightmare I live with all the time. Right now, for instance, the voices are telling me to go back and change the word "nightmare" to "living hell."

The voices torment me from the time I wake up. They'll say, "Get up and go to the bathroom to urinate."

Throughout the day, they never let up: "Go get something to eat," "Go take a nap," "Go to the bathroom again," "Get ready for bed." On and on. Sometimes the voices even talk to me in my sleep, telling me to get up and urinate. My fear is that the voices will tell me to do something crazy, like go look for a job.

I used to think that drinking alcohol would calm the voices, but it usually makes them worse. They'll say things like "Go tell that person what you really think of him" or "Get up on that table and do your funny cowboy dance."

The voices used to talk to me about the Beatles. When I was young, they'd tell me to go buy a certain Beatles album. "But I don't have any money," I'd say. Then the voices would suggest I mow some lawns to earn some money. "But that's a lot of work," I'd say. "Well," the voices would say, "do you want the album or not?" (Wait. That might have been my father.)

Sometimes I go for relatively long periods without the voices talking to me, such as when I'm watching TV, or watching ants, or lying on the floor and trying to blow lint balls into one big herd of lint. Or seeing which one of my cats is most afraid of "pillowcase head." But these golden moments are fleeting, and soon the voices return.

I just wish the voices would tell me something useful once in a while, like how to say things in French or where my gloves went. But they hardly ever do. In fact, many times the voices like to taunt me, telling me, for instance, to turn left at an intersection when, it turns out later, I clearly should have turned right. Or telling me to wear a tie that obviously looks ridiculous.

Even worse, sometimes the voices themselves don't know what they want. They'll tell me to go up and talk to a pretty woman, then they'll say, "No, wait, she's too pretty for you," then they'll say, "Oh, go ahead," then they'll say, "What if your wife finds out?" (Man, make up your mind!)

When you tell people you have voices in your head, they think you're crazy. But when you don't say anything at all, and you just sit there and stare at them, they also think you're crazy. So you can't win.

I thought about going to a psychiatrist to get rid of the voices, but the voices said it would be expensive, and would probably take a long time, and that I'd have to put my pants on and go to the subway, then come all the way back on the subway, then take my pants off, and who knows if it would even work? Sometimes the voices have a point.

One day, I decided that I couldn't take it anymore, and I decided to silence the voices in my head once and for all. But I couldn't figure out how to do that, so I never did.

Maybe the answer is not to try to get rid of the voices, but to learn to live with them. (I don't really think that; I'm just saying it for the voices.)

Will I ever be able to fully control the voices in my head? Probably not. But will I at least be able to adjust my lifestyle so that the voices are not a threat to me or others? Again, the answer is no.

But I'm not ready to throw in the towel just yet, because one thing I have learned is this: the voices may be bossy, but they're really stupid.

My Favorite Thing

It's not that much to look at. The nubs are completely worn off in some spots, the wooden prongs are swollen and warped, and the springs are so loose they can barely pull the magnets apart. And yet, I wouldn't trade it for anything. Every time I slip it out of its flannel tote bag, oil it up, and fasten down the straps, I feel like a king.

Like many of the best things, it's old. And rare—only a few thousand were ever made. Most of them, of course, went down with the *Titanic*. A few were mistakenly turned into bird feeders. And the rest have been avidly sought by museums, collectors, and "sportsmen."

I found mine many years ago in a run-down little shop in Asbestos, Colorado. The white-haired proprietor was bent over a table repairing it. Even with the rubber tubing, French grommets, and other parts scattered all over, I knew I had to have it. The old man sensed the light in my eyes and told me to come back in a week. I came back in two weeks, because, I don't know, I was busy or something, and paid the then princely sum of $58,000, plus my watch.

Since then, the shop has been bulldozed down, the old man has died (from a bulldozer), and Asbestos, Colorado, has changed its name to Aspen. But I still have my prize.

People ask me if it still works. That's like asking a Canadian if he likes puppets. It works like a dream, and not the kind where you wake up screaming.

Nowadays you can buy a modern, mass-produced version. And I admit, they're stronger, lighter, and much, much easier to turn off. But there's something about the originals that makes you want to hang on to them, at least until somebody makes you an offer of no less than $45,000.

Reintroducing Me
to My Habitat

I would like to take this opportunity to urge conservation-minded people everywhere to pressure the government for the reintroduction of me to my native habitat.

My native habitat, of course, is the desert Southwest, where I used to roam wild and free. But, sadly, I no longer exist there. For several years, I have been largely confined to a small two-bedroom apartment in the Chelsea section of Manhattan.

It is clear that I do not belong here, as my neighbors will tell you. I am still frightened by car horns, and the fancy Eastern food I am fed is at odds with my natural diet of enchiladas and ginger snaps. Often I can be found pacing mindlessly back and forth in my cramped office, which I am told is a sign that I am insane.

Occasionally, there are scattered sightings of me in my old habitat—shooting a wet straw wrapper at someone's kid in a restaurant in Santa Fe, then denying it; doing my funny cowboy dance at a party in Silver City until people make me stop—but these cannot be confirmed.

For all intents and purposes, I have been eliminated from my former range, the Rio Grande Valley. I used to be found from El Paso and Juárez in the south all the way up to Taos and sometimes beyond (if I missed the turnoff to Taos).

Once, I filled a vital role in the ecosystem. I would prey primarily on the weak and the old, who were usually the only ones who would hire me. Then, when their businesses went under, they were removed from the system, as nature intended.

My world was in harmony. But, as often happens, man intervened. Ranchers would drive me from their lands when they caught me throwing a keg-party barbecue, maybe using one of their cows. Divorce and job dismissals took their toll. I found I could not coexist with my creditors. At one point, public sentiment against me was so strong that I was considered "vermin" and a "pest."

But now, I think, attitudes are changing. People don't automatically want to shoot me, like they used to. This is mainly because of my reeducation efforts and because they haven't seen me for a long time.

The truth about me is finally starting to emerge. For instance, there is no record of me ever attacking a human, unless he was much, much smaller than me. The old myths are starting to die off, such as the one that if you leave your campsite unattended, I will sneak in and steal beer and food from your cooler and maybe knock down your tent.

The time to act is now. I am not getting any younger, and my rent here in New York could go up at any time. Also, I could be wiped out by the stock market.

I have been conducting a captive-breeding program with my wife, but so far it has yielded no offspring. (The reason, I found out, is that my wife uses contraceptives, which I guess I knew.)

All of these factors make it imperative that you write the government and tell them to reintroduce me, via first-class airfare, to my old habitat. With a generous per diem and a late-model car, I think I could once again fill my old niche. I would probably try to mate with females of my species, unless my wife found out. And I would be willing to keep a journal of what I eat and what TV shows I watch, so that more may be learned about my ways.

I will, if necessary, wear a radio collar.

I am willing to do these things because I believe that until people can sit around a desert campfire and go "Shhh, hear that?" and then listen for the plaintive howl of me, we as a society have lost something.

Tattoo

Recently, I got a sex change on a whim. I was out drinking with some friends, got really drunk, and went in for the surgery. The doctors suggested I wait until I was sober, but I said no, give me the sex change.

Well, to make a long story short (so to speak), I woke up with breasts, a vagina, and a splitting headache. Also, I had a tattoo. I don't remember where I got it, but there it was.

I was a woman for several weeks. The people at work were nice about it, but, to tell you the truth, I didn't really have time to enjoy being a woman—I was swamped with projects. Finally, I decided to go back to being a man. For one thing, I hadn't thought about how you need to change your whole wardrobe.

When I went in for the second surgery, I asked the doctor if he could also remove the tattoo while he was at it. He said, "But since you're going to be a man again, wouldn't you like to keep the tattoo?" I said no, man or woman, I didn't want the tattoo.

I woke up from the operation, and I was a man again. But get this: I still had the tattoo! I thought, Am I crazy? I confronted the surgeon, and he said he thought we had left the tattoo part undecided. Now that I was a man, I felt like punching him, but I didn't. Instead, I just made an appointment to come back and get the tattoo removed.

I should have been suspicious when I went back for the tattoo removal and they put me under full anesthesia, because when I woke up I was a woman again but *the tattoo was still there*! They said it had been a mistake, and to make up for it they would do my next surgery for free.

I didn't know what to do. I became depressed. I started getting hounded by my insurance company. They had covered my sex-change operations in full, but they said they didn't cover tattoo removal. But I didn't have a tattoo removed, I told them. They said they had already paid my doctor for one by mistake, and now I had to reimburse them. I called my doctor, and he said he hadn't received any payment for tattoo removal.

I was so mad, I felt like suing someone. But who? My drinking buddies didn't have any money, and I had no luck tracking down the tattoo parlor.

I gave up. I started hitting the bars and sleeping around. I don't even remember if I was a man or a woman at that point. I felt a little cheap, so maybe I was a woman.

Then one night, after some meaningless sex, I noticed a photo on my wall. It was Godzilla. And I thought, That was a pretty good movie, I should watch that again sometime. Then I saw another photo. It was me, without the tattoo. I looked so, so incomplete. Something clicked in my head, and in my gut or maybe my uterus. I hadn't realized it, but I liked the tattoo. I was a tattoo person!

I called my doctor and told him the news: I wanted to get another sex-change operation, but I was going to keep the tattoo. He said I was crazy. "Yeah," I said with a smirk, "crazy like Godzilla."

The Corrector

My dream job would be professional corrector. I would go around correcting people and things. For instance, if I saw you skiing down a mountain and I didn't think you were skiing very well, I would yell out a correction, like, "Hey, man, ski better!" Or, if you were fishing, I might call out, "Hey, don't just stand there, catch a fish!"

For yelling out a correction to someone, I would get five hundred dollars. For just shaking my head derisively and rolling my eyes, that would be only a hundred dollars. (So whoever's paying me for this dream job, you're getting a bargain right there.) I would also offer more detailed corrections, although I wouldn't actually do those myself. I would farm them out to a subcorrector. I would be only a general contractor.

But I wouldn't be in it for the money. In fact, I

would do this job for free.* My main joy would be in helping people. Let's say you're at the beach and you call out to a surfer: "Next time, try standing up the whole way, instead of falling over, like you just did." Imagine the satisfaction of seeing the guy do just that. Or imagine the pride you would feel when the winner of the Tour de France publicly thanked you for his victory, because you told him to "Pedal faster!"

I know I said earlier that I would not only correct people, but also "things." But I'm not sure how you could do that. How could you move a mountain a little more to the left, or make flowers redder, or frogs hoppier? Talk to God? Good luck with that. In my experience, that guy is always trying to correct *you*.

* This is not true.

How I Want to Be Remembered

We are gathered here, way far in the future, for the funeral of Jack Handey, the world's oldest man. He died suddenly in bed, according to his wife, Miss France.

No one is really sure how old Jack was, but some think he may have been born as long ago as the twentieth century. He passed away after a long and courageous battle with honky-tonkin' and alley cattin'.

Even though Jack was incredibly old, he was amazingly healthy right up to the end. He attributed this to performing his funny cowboy dance for friends, relatives, and people waiting for buses. All agreed it was the most hilarious thing they had ever seen, and not at all stupid or annoying.

Jack's death has thrown the whole world into mourning, and not in a fakey, sarcastic way. He was admired by people of all ages and stripes, and by all animals, including zebras. Even monsters liked him. He had had his playful side and his serious side, but 99 percent of the time he had his "normal" side.

He started out life as a baby but worked his way up to an adult. But even when he was a full-grown adult, he never forgot that he was a baby.

His philosophy of life was a simple one. "I'm-a no looka for trouble, because-a trouble, she's-a no good," he would often say in his beloved fake Italian accent. He was quick with a laugh, but just as quick to point at what he was laughing at. Children loved him, but not in the way his teenage niece claimed. He was always thinking of ways of helping people, and was wondering how he might do some of those things when he died.

Jack was an expert in so many fields, it's hard to say what he was best at: the arts, the sciences, or the businesses. If you talked to him at a party, you couldn't tell; he seemed to know it all. He has been compared to Captain James Cook, and not just because he was severely beaten by some Hawaiians, and to General Dwight D. Eisenhower, and not just because he liked to be driven around in a jeep.

As hard as it is to believe, he never sold a single painting during his lifetime, or even painted one. Some of the greatest advances in architecture, medicine, and theater were not opposed by him, and he did little to sabotage them.

Although he lived in Paris, in a mansion famous for its many trap doors, he was always proud to be an American. However, he was ashamed to be an Earthling.

He was fabulously wealthy, but he would pretend to be broke, and would often try to borrow cigarettes and money from people. Little did they know that those who gave him stuff would later be rewarded in his will, with jewels and anti-gravity helmets. Women who refused to have sex with him are probably wishing that they could turn back the clock and say yes.

Generous even with his organs, he has asked that his eyes be donated to a blind person. Also his glasses. His skeleton, equipped with a spring that will suddenly propel it to full height, will be used to educate kindergartners.

He has asked that no shrines be built to him. But he pointed out that this did not mean he didn't like Shriners.

According to our scientists, with their electronic soul trackers, Jack is in Heaven now. And not just regular Heaven, which any jerk can get in to, but special secret Heaven that even some angels don't know about.

So let us celebrate his death, and not mourn. However, those who appear to be a little too happy will be asked to leave.

Perhaps the greatest tragedy is that a lot of the things Jack said and did seemed wrong at the time, but now we realize it wasn't him, it was we who were wrong. Let us hope we don't make the same mistake with his clones.

In closing, it is unfortunate that Jack's friend Don could not be here. However, Don died many years ago, from a horrible fungus.

And now, robot Elton John will play "Candle in the Wind."

Television *Sketches*

Deer Heads

(A sportsman's study. A sportsman [Harvey Keitel] *chews on a cigar and holds a Tom Collins. He stands next to a deer head mounted on a wall.)*

SPORTSMAN

Hi. Welcome to my deer heads. This first
deer is a real beauty, as you can see. Big fella.
Ten-pointer. I got him about three years ago.
(Sportsman moves down the wall to the next deer head,
which is smaller)
. . . This is a smaller one I shot the next year.
(He moves to next deer head, which is smaller)
. . . This is a baby deer.
(He moves to the next deer head, even smaller.)
. . . And this one is the baby of *that* deer.
(He refers to previous baby deer, then proceeds to the
next deer head, which is even smaller)

. . . This is a little miniature deer I got as a pet.
I got tired of it and shot it.

(Moves to even smaller deer head)

. . . Now this little freak deer. A scientist friend
of mine developed it. The thing was actually killed
by the automatic tennis ball server.

(Moves on to next tiny mounted head)

. . . This is a mouse. A friend of mine asked me if
it was a deer mouse. *(Laughs)* I said, "I don't know,
but it'd be funny if it was, though!"

(Coughs, then comes to a little plastic deer head)

. . . This is what we call a toy deer.
I bought it at Toys "R" Us and cut its head off
and stuck it up there.

(Moves to next wall mount)

. . . This is a really big ant I found.

(Moves on to three little mounts in a row)

. . . And these are its eggs.

(Comes to a microscope mounted on the wall)

. . . Now, this, I don't know if you can get your
camera in there or not . . .

(Camera "looks" in microscope)

. . . Go ahead and look in there . . .

(Dissolve to a microscope slide of germs)

. . . In the upper left-hand corner—you see that
thing? That is a deer. Or at least that's my theory.
And if I can get my hands on one of those electron

scalpels, or whatever you call them, I think I can
cut its head off.

(Sportsman looks at his empty glass)

Well, it looks like I need a refill.

(He walks over to the bar and makes himself a drink)

ANNOUNCER

This has been "An Insane Idiot and His
Collection of Descending-Sized Deer Heads."

(Fade)

Broadcast Jan. 16, 1993

Anne Boleyn

(A cell in the Tower of London. Anne Boleyn [Candice Bergen] *looks wistfully out the barred window. Lord Norfolk* [Phil Hartman] *enters and bows.)*

ANNE BOLEYN

Oh, Norfolk! Pray, what news from my beloved husband, the king?

LORD NORFOLK

It bodes ill, Your Majesty. The king . . . demands your death.

ANNE BOLEYN

(shaken)

I feared as much. What manner of execution is it to be?

LORD NORFOLK

The choosing is yours, my lady.

ANNE BOLEYN

How so, Norfolk?

LORD NORFOLK

If you grant the king a divorce, and renounce
any claim to the throne, you shall be beheaded.
If you do not, then you shall . . . be burned at
the stake.

(Anne Boleyn weighs this)

ANNE BOLEYN

After I am beheaded, what will happen to my head?

LORD NORFOLK

It will be placed on top of a wall for public display.
People will be allowed to throw things at it in
attempts to knock it off the wall.

ANNE BOLEYN

How many throws will each person get before
another person gets to throw?

LORD NORFOLK

Three.

ANNE BOLEYN

Will they be allowed to throw anything?

LORD NORFOLK

Within reason.

ANNE BOLEYN

Would a rotten potato be considered reasonable?

LORD NORFOLK

I'm afraid it would, Your Majesty.

ANNE BOLEYN

But I mean a really rotten one, all mushy and such.
(Norfolk nods reluctantly)

ANNE BOLEYN

And when my head is knocked off the wall, will
the dirt and mud be brushed off my face before
it is set back on the wall?

LORD NORFOLK

I am not sure, Your Majesty. I will inquire.

ANNE BOLEYN

Thank you, Norfolk.

LORD NORFOLK

I will leave you now, to weigh your decision.
(Norfolk bows deeply and heads for the door)

ANNE BOLEYN

(after him)
Norfolk.

LORD NORFOLK

Yes, Your Majesty?

ANNE BOLEYN

What if I grant the divorce, renounce the throne,
but invoke the blessing of the pope?

LORD NORFOLK

Then you shall be drawn and quartered by four
large horses. Then the quarters shall be drawn
and quartered by four smaller horses. Then those
quarters will be drawn and quartered by four
frogs. After that, the quartering would stop and
the mincing would begin.

ANNE BOLEYN

I see. And my head?

LORD NORFOLK

Your head would be placed on a pike.

ANNE BOLEYN

On a fish, Norfolk?

LORD NORFOLK

No, Your Majesty, a "spike" pike.

ANNE BOLEYN

(alarmed)

Oh, Norfolk! What about the crows? Would they not attack my face?

LORD NORFOLK

We would put a wire cage over your head. It would keep out the crows, but smaller birds would be able to shoulder their way through the bars.

ANNE BOLEYN

And I suppose yellow jackets could get through?

LORD NORFOLK

Yes, Your Majesty.

ANNE BOLEYN

And June bugs?

LORD NORFOLK

Yes. But June bugs wouldn't really do any harm. They just sort of crawl around on your face . . .

(Norfolk illustrates)

ANNE BOLEYN

Could a small scarecrow be attached to my forehead?

LORD NORFOLK

Again, I will inquire into the matter, Your Majesty.
But now, I will take my leave.
(Norfolk bows and starts to exit)

ANNE BOLEYN

Norfolk?

LORD NORFOLK

(a little wearily)
Yes, Your Majesty.

ANNE BOLEYN

What if I just do everything they ask?

LORD NORFOLK

In that case, your head will be chopped off,
and then it will be shot out of a cannon.

ANNE BOLEYN

How many times?

LORD NORFOLK

I'm not sure. It seems to be really arbitrary.

ANNE BOLEYN

And my body?

LORD NORFOLK

It would be folded up and also shot out of a cannon.

ANNE BOLEYN

Would my head ever be shot *at* my body?

LORD NORFOLK

It might, Your Majesty.

ANNE BOLEYN

Yewww! What happens to my head after that?

LORD NORFOLK

It would be wrapped up like a present and sent
anonymously to a stranger. The royal entourage
would hide in the bushes to see the expression
on the stranger's face when he opened it.

ANNE BOLEYN

Norfolk, you may inform the king I have made
my decision: I will grant the divorce, renounce the
throne, and have my head . . . cut off.

LORD NORFOLK

Very well, Your Majesty. Now, is that the one where
we put your head on the wall? I'm lost.

ANNE BOLEYN

Yes, that's the one.

LORD NORFOLK

I will take my leave now, Your Majesty.
(He bows)

ANNE BOLEYN

Norfolk?

LORD NORFOLK

Yes, Your Majesty.

ANNE BOLEYN

The executioner—is he skilled?

LORD NORFOLK

Very skilled, madam. He has been sent for
from Calais.
*(Execution room. Norfolk and the assembled members
of the court are spattered with blood from off-camera.
Ax thuds.)*

ANNE BOLEYN

(off-camera)

YOWWWWWWW!!!! OWWW!!
WOWWWWWW!! OHHH-YEOWWWW!!!
WHOA, MAMA!!!!

ANNOUNCER

The execution of Anne Boleyn took six and a
half hours and three axes, and was one of the
bloodiest in royal history. At one point, Anne
Boleyn cried out that she would rather be burned
at the stake, but it was decided to carry on. Later,
her head was placed atop a pike, which swam
away, never to be seen again.

(Fade)

Broadcast Nov. 21, 1987

Unfrozen Cave
Man Lawyer

(Bleak, frozen wasteland)

ANNOUNCER

One hundred thousand years ago, a cave man was
out hunting on the frozen wastes when he slipped
and fell into a crevasse. In 1988, he was discovered
by some scientists and thawed out. He then went to
law school and became . . . Unfrozen Cave Man
Lawyer!

(A thick-skulled cave man [Phil Hartman] *makes a
demonstrative hitting motion with a stone ax.
Dissolve to cave man in same pose in courtroom, in
Brooks Brothers suit, making similar motion with
his hand.)*

SONG

HE USED TO BE A CAVE MAN
BUT NOW HE'S A LAWYER
UNFROZEN CAVE MAN LAWYER

ANNOUNCER

Brought to you by . . .

(Shot of lovable dog with rifle sight superimposed)

. . . Dog Assassin. "When you can't bear
to put him to sleep, maybe it's time to call
Dog Assassin."

(Shot of foot-long pinto bean on a plate)

And by Big Fat Bean. "Why eat hundreds
of little beans when you can eat one big one?"
And now, tonight's episode of *Unfrozen Cave Man
Lawyer* . . .

(Courtroom. Cave man lawyer sits at table.
He wears a suit, but still has scraggly hair and
thick Neanderthal brow. However, he speaks glibly.)

JUDGE

Mister Kee-Rok, are you ready to give
your summation?

CAVE MAN LAWYER

It's just Kee-Rok, your honor. And yes,
I'm ready. *(Approaches jury)* Ladies and
gentlemen of the jury, I'm just a cave man.

I fell in some ice and then got thawed out by
your scientists. Your world frightens and
confuses me. Sometimes the honking horns of
your traffic make me want to get out of my
BMW and run off, into the hills or whatever.
When I get a message on my fax machine, I
wonder, did little demons get inside and type it?
I don't know. My primitive brain can't grasp
these concepts.
(Judge is annoyed)

CAVE MAN LAWYER
But I do know this: whatever world you're from,
when a man like my client . . .
(Client has sad face and phony-looking bandages)

CAVE MAN LAWYER
. . . slips and falls on a sidewalk in front of a
public library, he should receive no less than
two million dollars in compensatory damages
and two million dollars in punitive damages.
Thank you.
(Jury members are impressed)

JUDGE
The jury will now retire to deliberate.

JURY FOREMAN

Your honor, we don't need to retire. Kee-Rok's
words are just as true now as they were in
his time. We give him the full amount!
(Jury members nod and applaud)

JUDGE

Did you hear that, Mister Kee-Rok?
(Cave man lawyer is on cell phone)

CAVE MAN LAWYER

I'm sorry, Your Honor. I was listening to the
magic voices coming out of this strange modern
invention.

ANNOUNCER

This has been *Unfrozen Cave Man Lawyer.*
Join us next week for another episode. Here's
a scene . . .
*(Film of airliner. Inside plane, cave man
is drunk. He stops a flight attendant
carrying several trays.)*

CAVE MAN LAWYER

(drunk)
Stewardess, could you get me another drink?

FLIGHT ATTENDANT

I'm sorry, sir, but the chief steward says you've already had enough.

CAVE MAN LAWYER

But you don't understand. I'm a cave man.
I'm frightened by your strange flying machine.
So bring me another Dewar's and water,
pronto.

FLIGHT ATTENDANT

I'm sorry, sir.

(Exits)

CAVE MAN LAWYER

(after her)

I'll sue you and your whole goddam airline!

ANNOUNCER

. . . Next time, on *Unfrozen Cave Man Lawyer*!

(Fade)

Broadcast Nov. 23, 1991

Toonces, the Cat Who Could Drive a Car

(Head-on shot of a cat [live cat with fake paws] driving a car.)

SONG
TOONCES, THE DRIVING CAT
THE CAT WHO COULD DRIVE A CAR
HE DRIVES AROUND
ALL OVER THE TOWN
TOONCES, THE DRIVING CAT!

ANNOUNCER
Toonces, the Cat Who Could Drive a Car.
(A housewife [Victoria Jackson] is cooking as her husband [Steve Martin] enters excitedly.)

HUSBAND
Honey, you won't believe it! Toonces can drive a car!

WIFE

Toonces, our cat?

HUSBAND

That's right! Come on, I'll show you!
(*Car driving on a mountain road. Sound of swerving
tires. Inside car, a cat puppet is "driving" the car.
Husband and wife sit alongside.*)

HUSBAND

See, I told you he could drive.

WIFE

Toonces, look out!
(*Stock footage of car going over a cliff and crashing*)
(*Husband and wife, hair and clothes mussed, stagger
over to a log and sit.*)

WIFE

I thought you said he could drive!

HUSBAND

I thought he could. I saw him up there fooling
around with the steering wheel, and I guess
I just *assumed* he could drive.

WIFE

That's okay, honey. Anybody would think that.
(*Sound of car starting up and driving off*)

HUSBAND

Hey, look! He's driving away!

WIFE

I guess he can drive.

HUSBAND

Yeah. Just not very well.

SONG

HE DRIVES AROUND

ALL OVER THE TOWN

TOONCES, THE DRIVING CAT!

ANNOUNCER

Next on *Toonces, the Cat Who Could Drive a Car*:
"The Driving Test."
(Wife is cooking as husband frets)

WIFE

Do you think Toonces will pass his driving test?

HUSBAND

I don't know. The written part is pretty hard.
And he can't even read.

WIFE

Maybe he'll make it up on the driving part.

HUSBAND

Damn, I just wish I could help him!
(Police officer [Kevin Nealon] in the front seat of car.
  Toonces is behind the wheel)

POLICEMAN

(to cat)

All right, sir, if you'll just go ahead and pull out
into traffic . . .

(Car suddenly accelerates)

POLICEMAN

LOOK OUT!!!

(Car flies off cliff)

SONG

TOONCES, THE DRIVING CAT!

(Fade)

Broadcast May 20, 1989

Happy Fun Ball

*(Three exuberant young people chase a hard rubber
ball down a suburban sidewalk. They are having way
too much fun. Boing-boing-boing sound effects.
Ventures guitar music.)*

YOUNG WOMAN
(excited)
It's happy!

YOUNG MAN
It's fun!

ALL THREE
It's Happy Fun Ball!
(Super: Happy Fun Ball)

ANNOUNCER

Yes, It's Happy Fun Ball! The toy sensation
that's sweeping the nation!
(Product shot of Happy Fun Ball. Flashing "$14.95")

ANNOUNCER

Only fourteen ninety-five, at participating
stores! Get one today!
(Super the following warnings as announced:)

ANNOUNCER

(more serious)

Warning: Pregnant women, the elderly, and
children under ten should avoid prolonged
exposure to Happy Fun Ball.

. . . Caution: Happy Fun Ball may suddenly
accelerate to dangerous speeds.

. . . Happy Fun Ball contains a liquid core, which,
if exposed due to rupture, should not be touched,
inhaled, or looked at.

. . . Do not use Happy Fun Ball on concrete.

. . . Discontinue use of Happy Fun Ball if any of
the following occurs:

- Itching
- Vertigo
- Dizziness
- Tingling in extremities

(Super turns to crawl:)

- Loss of balance or coordination
- Slurred speech
- Temporary blindness
- Sudden hair loss
- Chattering teeth
- Heart palpitations

(Super:)

. . . If Happy Fun Ball begins to smoke, get away immediately. Seek shelter and cover head.

. . . Happy Fun Ball may stick to certain types of skin.

. . . When not in use, Happy Fun Ball should be returned to its special container and kept under refrigeration. Failure to do so relieves the makers of Happy Fun Ball, Wacky Products Incorporated, and its parent company, Global Chemical Unlimited, of any and all liability.

. . . Ingredients of Happy Fun Ball include an unknown glowing substance which fell to Earth, presumably from outer space.

. . . Happy Fun Ball has been shipped to our troops in Saudi Arabia and is also being dropped by our warplanes in Iraq.

. . . Do not taunt Happy Fun Ball.

. . . Happy Fun Ball comes with a
lifetime guarantee.

(happier)

Happy Fun Ball!

(Super: Happy Fun Ball)

. . . Accept no substitutes!

(Fade)

Broadcast Feb. 16, 1991

The Zombies vs. the Bees

(Two lovers [Dana Carvey, Victoria Jackson]
*in a car on isolated lovers' lane. Dark, scary
woods. Girl breaks the kiss.)*

BOY

What's the matter?

GIRL

I don't know. I feel like
somebody's watching us.

BOY

Oh, come on.
*(They resume kissing. A zombie peers out from
behind a bush.)*

GIRL

(breaking kiss)

There. I heard something. Didn't
you hear that?

BOY

I didn't hear anything. Come on,
Wendy, it's nothing.

GIRL

Are you sure?

BOY

Positive.

*(Resume kissing. A group of zombies,
arms outstretched, break out from the
bushes, stagger toward car)*

(Girl spots them and screams)

BOY

Oh, my God, what are they?

GIRL

They're zombies! Let's get out
of here!

*(Car won't start. Zombies get
closer. They're hideous)*

GIRL

Jeff, start the car!

BOY

It won't start! We're going to have
to make a run for it!
*(Zombies suddenly stop, then wave their arms, trying to
ward off an attack of bees. Buzzing sounds.)*

BOY

Wait! Something's happening.

GIRL

They're being attacked . . . by bees.
(Super: The Zombies vs. the Bees)
(Dramatic sci-fi music)
(Zombies, tormented by the bees, flail about)

*(Sheriff's office. Sheriff [Carl Weathers] talks
to shaken boy and girl.)*

SHERIFF

Now, tell me again what happened.

GIRL

There were these zombies stalking us.
Then, all of a sudden, they were attacked
by swarms of bees.

BOY

It was horrible, Sheriff.

SHERIFF

Well, what do you want me to do about it?

BOY

Shouldn't we get involved somehow?

SHERIFF

Why? Who cares? It's zombies and bees.
Let them work it out.

*(A zombie appears outside the window. He's
being attacked by bees. He howls and flails
about.)*

DEPUTY

Sheriff, there's a zombie outside
being attacked by bees. Should I let him in?

SHERIFF

No, he might eat us. Plus, he'll just bring
those bees in with him.

*(Laboratory. Scientist [Nora Dunn] looks at a
glowing liquid in a beaker. She phones.
Sheriff answers.)*

SCIENTIST

Sheriff, this is Professor Blanston. I've done it!
I've succeeded in creating an ointment that
will protect zombies from bee stings.

SHERIFF

So?

SCIENTIST

Well, aren't we on the side of the zombies?

SHERIFF

No. Why would we be?

SCIENTIST

Well, they're sort of humanoid, aren't they?

SHERIFF

Yes, but they're unnatural. They're from
the grave. If we took any side, I think it would
be the bees. They're more of a normal-type
creature.

SCIENTIST

But they sting.

SHERIFF

Look, I'm not going to argue with you.

SCIENTIST

So what should I do with this ointment?

SHERIFF

Boy, you got me. I guess just throw it out.
(Sheriff hangs up. Deputy approaches.)

DEPUTY

Sir, I just received a report that
piranhas have joined the war on the side
of the zombies.

SHERIFF

Yeah? What does that mean?

DEPUTY

Well, basically, if any bees land on water
infested with piranhas, the piranhas will attack
them.

SHERIFF

Big deal. Who cares? Look, I'm gonna go
play golf.
*(Shot of zombies outdoors, stumbling about, swatting at
  bees.)*

ANNOUNCER

The zombies and the bees continued their war for several more years, until finally, a peace treaty was signed. A representative of the humans was invited to attend the signing, but failed to show up.

(Super: The End)

(Fade)

Produced Jan. 27, 1988—never broadcast